Drug Testing

An Issue for School, Sports, and Work

Drug Testing

An Issue for School, Sports, and Work

David E. Newton

Enslow Publishers, Inc.

40 Industrial Road   PO Box 38
Box 398   Aldershot
Berkeley Heights, NJ 07922   Hants GU12 6BP
USA   UK

http://www.enslow.com

For Victoria Stillman, with many memories of both
good times and hard times.

Library of Congress Cataloging-in-Publication Data

Newton, David E.
  Drug testing: an issue for school, sports, and work / David E. Newton.
      p.   cm. — (Issues in focus)
  Includes bibliographical references and index.
  Summary: Examines differing opinions on the topic of drug testing by
employers, in schools, and in sports as a means of curbing drug abuse.
  ISBN 0-89490-954-1
  1. Employees—Drug testing—United States—Juvenile literature.
  [1. Drug testing.] I. Title. II. Series: Issues in focus (Springfield, N.J.)
  HF5549.5.D7N493   1999
  658.3'822—dc21   98-21607
                                                  CIP
                                                  AC
Printed in the United States of America

10 9 8 7 6 5 4 3 2

To Our Readers:
All Internet addresses in this book were active and appropriate when we
went to press. Any comments or suggestions can be sent by e-mail to
Comments@enslow.com or to the address on the back cover.

Illustration Credits: © Corel Corporation, pp. 9, 90; LabCorp
Occupational Testing Services, p. 69; National Clearinghouse for
Alcohol and Drug Information, pp. 41, 75, 79; Nationwide Truckers
Association, Inc., p. 43; David E. Newton, pp. 25, 98; OML
Laboratories, p. 37; PMI Incorporated, p. 62; Courtesy of SmithKline
Beecham Clinical Laboratories, pp. 21, 57; Courtesy of U.S. Army, p.
27; Courtesy of U.S. Department of Agriculture, p. 15; Courtesy of
U.S. Department of the Interior, p. 51; Courtesy of U.S. Food and
Drug Administration, p. 59; Courtesy of World Health Organization,
p. 47.

Cover Illustration: © Corel Corporation.

Contents

1

The Drug Problem in the United States

On January 4, 1987, an Amtrak train and a Conrail train collided near Chase, Maryland. In the accident, 16 people were killed and 170 more were injured. The total financial cost to the two railway systems was estimated at $100 million. Investigators found that the engineer of the Conrail train had smoked marijuana before beginning his run. He ran through three stop signals before the collision occurred. The engineer's use of marijuana was discovered when he was subjected to a mandatory drug test following the accident.[1]

. . . .

In a testimonial on the benefits of workplace drug testing, the employer of

7

thirty people at a structural steel plant in Florida states the following:

> This year we will spend $1,500 to run the [drug testing] program and will save about $35,000, primarily in workers' comp[ensation] premiums. . . . There is no question we have a higher caliber workforce today. . . . I simply don't understand why any company would hesitate to have a drug-free workplace. . . . It's the right thing to do, and it's financially beneficial, too.[2]

Drug use in the workplace is a serious problem in the United States today, and drug testing is one way to deal with that issue. It appears that many Americans have accepted that argument. In 1995, the Gallup Organization conducted a survey on the nation's most serious problems. Over half (57 percent) of all respondents ranked drug abuse "nine" or "ten" on a scale of one to ten in importance. Just under 10 percent called drug abuse "the most important problem facing the nation today." That percentage had remained at the 5- to 10-percent level for more than a decade.[3]

There are many kinds of problems associated with illegal drug use. For example, many drug users resort to burglary, prostitution, or other illegal activities to get the money they need to maintain their drug habits. Also, those who sell drugs sometimes wage all-out wars to protect their "turf," the neighborhoods in which they conduct their business. In addition, intravenous drug use is a major source of HIV infections and other health problems.

For many Americans, however, the greatest cause of concern about illegal drug use is the problems it creates in the workplace. People who use illegal drugs may represent a threat to the general public whom they serve. The railroad engineer described in the first anecdote above is an example. Similarly, the thought of an airplane pilot using cocaine just before takeoff is frightening to anyone.

Drug users may also represent less obvious risks to their coworkers and to the general public. The assembly-line worker who comes to the job slightly confused after smoking a marijuana cigarette may

A number of jobs require employees to perform precise operations without margin for error.

make errors in his or her work that are difficult to detect until much later in the production process. Or a drug user may miss many days of work while recovering from the aftereffects of drug use. Employers such as the one mentioned in the second anecdote above continue to look for ways to reduce the risks to their businesses created by illegal drug users.

Another View

Many people, however, strongly oppose the concept of testing for drugs in the workplace. They point out that two of the most serious problems in the nation today are the use of alcohol and the use of tobacco products, both of which are *legal* drugs. The engineer in the 1987 accident, for example, had a blood alcohol content higher than that permitted by law. In addition, opponents of drug testing say, many businesspeople are themselves opposed to drug testing. They do not believe that the costs of testing are justified by the results produced. Although drug testing detects recent drug use, it does not show whether an employee is presently impaired and thus unable to perform job functions. Finally, many people believe that drug testing is an invasion of personal privacy.

For more than three decades, Americans have struggled with the issue of illegal drug use. The search for effective ways of dealing with the problem continues today. Testing has become one of the most popular and widely used techniques for detecting drug abuse. Serious debate still rages, however, about the effectiveness, reliability, and ethics of workplace drug testing. This book attempts to give each side in the issue of drug testing an opportunity to present its case. As you read each chapter and section of the book, be aware that every argument has at least two sides. There is always more to a discussion than appears at first glance!

2

Testing for
Illegal Drugs

A medical dictionary defines a drug as "any substance that when taken into the living organism may modify one or more of its functions."[1] That definition includes a wide range of materials, including aspirin, milk of magnesia, penicillin, caffeine, alcohol, marijuana, and cocaine. When people talk about "drug abuse," however, they are referring to only those drugs that are illegal to use without a doctor's prescription or that are illegal to use under any circumstances whatsoever. Such drugs are also called *illicit* drugs. Examples of illicit drugs include cocaine,

12

heroin, marijuana, PCP (phencyclidine), and hallucinogens, such as LSD (lysergic acid diethylamine) and peyote. For young people, two other widely used drugs—alcohol and tobacco—are also illegal. These drugs are, of course, legal for adults to use.

Illicit Drugs

The Comprehensive Drug Abuse Control Act of 1970 (also called the Controlled Substance Act) provides guidelines for classifying drugs. The act creates five categories, or schedules, for drugs. The categories define the likelihood of misuse of a drug and the risk associated with that misuse. For example, drugs in Schedule I have no approved medical uses and high potentials for abuse by individuals. Some of the best-known Schedule I drugs are marijuana, heroin, and LSD. At the present time, though, there is an active debate about possible medical uses for marijuana. In 1997, two states—Arizona and California—adopted laws that permit the use of marijuana for certain specific medical purposes.

Schedule II drugs have some medical uses but high potential risks for users. Cocaine, morphine, and methamphetamine are examples of Schedule II drugs. These drugs do have medical applications (as in the control of pain) but pose high risks of addiction and psychological damage to users.

Interestingly enough, the two drugs that present the greatest potential threat in the workplace, in schools, and among professional athletes are not illegal. These are nicotine (an important component of tobacco products) and alcohol. The Substance Abuse and Mental Health Services Administration (SAMHSA) conducts an annual National Household Survey on Drug Abuse. Its 1996 survey found that the number of people who reported using alcohol in the preceding month (109.1 million) and those who reported using some form of tobacco (61.8 million) far exceeded the number who had used marijuana or hashish (10.1 million), cocaine (1.7 million), or any other form of illicit drug, including inhalants, hallucinogens, PCP, LSD, and heroin (5.8 million).[2] Yet, since nicotine and alcohol are not illegal for adults to use, they are not considered in this book.

Drug Use and Abuse

Many drugs are valuable because of their medical benefits. Morphine, for example, is one of the most powerful painkillers known to science. People in advanced stages of some forms of cancer depend on morphine to obtain relief from their most serious episodes of pain. When used properly, morphine is a great benefit to the medical profession and to people who are ill.

But morphine can also be used improperly; it can be *abused*. An unfortunate side effect of morphine use is that one can become addicted to the drug. Addiction means that a person experiences an intense craving for a substance and feels unable to live without continued use of the drug. People who take morphine as a way of reducing pain may

Marijuana, a Schedule I drug, may have medical uses.

become addicted to the drug. They might continue to take the drug even after all pain has disappeared.

The "drug problem" with which Americans are concerned, then, really has two parts. One part involves the *misuse* of legal and potentially valuable drugs, such as codeine and morphine. The second part involves the *use* of illegal drugs with no medical value, such as LSD and heroin.

Drug Testing in the Workplace

Who is the typical user of illegal drugs? Perhaps you think first of a homeless man or woman who spends the little money he or she has to support a drug

...1 fact, research indicates that 74 percent ...11cit drug users are employed in full-time jobs. ...n one study, 15.4 percent of all construction workers between the ages of eighteen and thirty-four admitted to having used illegal drugs at some time in their lives. That rate is the highest of any occupation in the United States. By comparison, 9 percent of all transportation workers and 8.1 percent of manufacturing workers admitted to using illegal drugs.[3]

Proponents of drug testing in the workplace use the statistics to support their position. Testing, they say, can be a crucial part of the nation's effort to solve its illegal drug problem. If we can identify those individuals who are employed and are using drugs, they argue, we will have identified three quarters of the nation's illicit drug users.

Critics of drug testing present a different view of this argument. Although testing may identify drug users, they say, it will not necessarily identify those individuals who are unable to perform their jobs properly. Thus, testing actually turns employers into "drug war police" and creates an unhealthy atmosphere in the workplace.

Methods of Drug Testing

A drill-press operator shows up for work looking as if he is unwell. His supervisor suspects that he has been using an illegal drug and asks the worker to take a drug test. What kind of experience can the drill-press operator expect during that drug test?

Drugs that have been introduced into the human

body can be detected in urine, blood, other body fluids, and in hair. By far, though, the most common type of drug test is urinalysis. During urinalysis, a person is asked to urinate into a specimen bottle. In most cases, a supervisor watches the collection of urine, either in person or in secret. The urine sample is then examined with chemical tests. The chemical test may be able to detect an illegal drug itself. More commonly, however, it detects a chemical produced during the breakdown of the drug in the body.

Any matter that enters the human body (including a drug) undergoes chemical changes. As an example, foods are broken down by the digestive system into simple sugars, amino acids, and other substances. These substances are then used by cells to manufacture energy and new compounds needed by the body, such as proteins. The substances formed during this breakdown process are known as metabolites. Most drug tests detect drug metabolites, not drugs themselves. The importance of this point for drug testing in the workplace is that a urine test typically shows what drugs were used at some time in the recent past, a few hours or a few days earlier. That drug use may have taken place during a person's private, nonworking time. It may tell little or nothing about the person's present ability to do his or her job.

The human body takes different periods of time to break down and eliminate different substances. For example, amphetamines and their metabolites can be detected by drug tests for a period of about forty-eight hours after they were ingested, but not much longer. A person who has taken amphetamines at 8 P.M. on Monday will probably test positive for the drug until Wednesday evening, but no later. Table 1 summarizes the periods during which various drugs can be detected. The data in this table are not absolute; studies sometimes show different figures for the lifetimes of various drugs.

A number of techniques are available for testing for drug metabolites. The test most commonly used today is the enzyme-multiplied immunoassay technique (EMIT). In an EMIT test, a sample of urine is mixed with a chemical. The chemical combines with drug metabolites in the sample. The combination of chemical and drug metabolite produces a distinctive color. The presence of the color therefore shows that a drug metabolite is present. Another test that was once very popular and is easier to understand than EMIT is thin-layer chromatography (TLC). In TLC, a urine sample is mixed with other chemicals and passed down a thin strip of filter paper. Metabolites in the urine sample separate out as spots on the paper strip. The presence of an "amphetamine spot" on the paper indicates the presence of an amphetamine metabolite in the urine sample.

One problem with TLC is that it may produce incorrect conclusions. It may indicate the presence of a drug metabolite when that drug is not actually present (a false positive). Or it may indicate that no drug metabolite is present when it actually is in the sample (a false negative).

TABLE 1: Detectability of Various Drugs in Urine[4]	
DRUG	**PERIOD OF DETECTABILITY**
amphetamine/methamphetamine ("pep pills," "speed," "ice," "meth")	48 hrs.
barbiturates ("downers," "yellow jackets," "red devils")	
short-acting	24 hrs.
intermediate-acting	48–72 hrs.
long-acting	7+ days
cocaine ("coke," "snow")	48–72 hrs.
marijuana ("pot," "grass," "Mary Jane," "MJ")	
single use	3 days
moderate use (4 times/week)	4 days
heavy use (daily)	10 days
chronic heavy use	21–27 days
methaqualone (quaaludes)	7+ days
phencyclidine (PCP, "angel dust")	8 days

False positives and false negatives may occur for a variety of reasons, such as the presence of chemicals in urine that act like drug metabolites, human error, or simply because chemical tests are not perfect. For these reasons, any urine sample that produces a positive test for an illicit drug is tested a second time, using a different test. The confirmatory test is much more accurate than TLC or other preliminary tests. However, it also tends to cost more. The most common confirmatory test is known as a gas chromatography/mass spectrometry (GC/MS) test, which has a high degree of accuracy. A GC/MS test is somewhat similar to a TLC test. A urine sample is mixed with a gas and passed through a detection chamber. Any drug metabolites in the sample are separated out. The metabolites are then passed through a second device, a mass spectrometer, that confirms the presence of the metabolites. It shows which metabolites are present in the sample.

In the early days of drug testing, false results were common. In 1985, the Centers for Disease Control conducted a review of drug testing results from 1972 to 1981. It found false positive rates as high as 66 percent and false negative rates as high as 100 percent.[5] The high rates of false positives and false negatives with TLC have led to the greater reliance on EMIT testing today.

The rates of false positives and false negatives have decreased as drug testing procedures have improved. One study of thirty-one laboratories conducted by the American Association of Clinical Chemists, for example, found only 3 percent false negatives and no false positives.[6] Critics of testing point out, however, that improvements in drug testing do not mean that the number of incorrect results have fallen to zero. That goal is probably not achievable in the real world. This problem can be

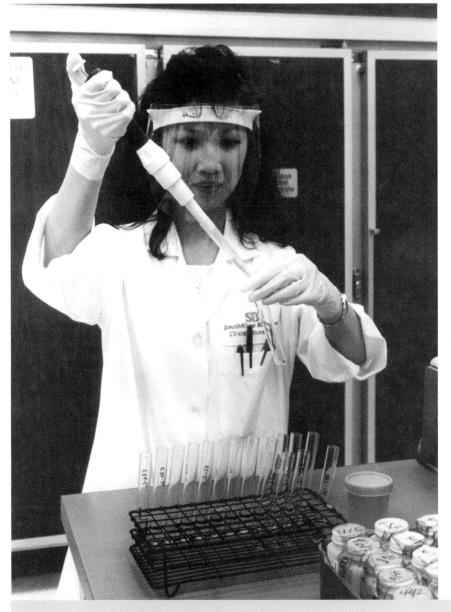

A technologist prepares a urine sample for drug testing.

especially severe during preemployment testing. Many companies demand that applicants take a drug test during the application process. If they fail that test, they probably will not be hired. In such cases, no follow-up tests are conducted, and no false results are likely to be discovered.

Advances in Drug Testing Technology

Scientists are always looking for improvements on urinalysis for drug testing. Their efforts are aimed at finding methods that are accurate, inexpensive, and less embarrassing and degrading than "peeing in a cup." One suggestion has been to use hair samples for drug testing.

Hair can be used in testing for drugs because chemicals taken into the body are generally incorporated into growing hair. A substance can first be detected about a week after ingestion and will remain in the hair for many weeks or months. As the hair grows, it carries with it any chemicals that have been ingested. Thus, a single strand of hair becomes a time line that shows the chemicals that have been ingested and the time they were taken into the body.

Experts point out a number of advantages of hair testing over urinalysis. First, hair is easier to handle and store than urine. Second, hair can be tested for the presence of drugs taken over a much longer period of time. Third, a person who stops taking drugs in anticipation of a drug test will not be able to "fool" the hair test. Finally, a hair sample is easier and less degrading for the subject to provide than a urine sample.[7]

Hair testing has a number of disadvantages too, though. For example, the procedure only indicates drug use after a fairly long period of time, after hair has had a chance to grow. Someone using an illicit drug today would not produce a positive hair test result for many days or weeks. Also, people who have been in the presence of someone smoking marijuana may test positive for the drug because the smoke contaminated their hair. In general, many scientists and regulators are still not convinced that hair testing is a valid technique for detection of drugs.

Another form of drug testing that may achieve the necessary goals without the limitations of urinalysis uses a person's perspiration, or sweat. In 1995, the United States Food and Drug Administration approved the sale of the first sweat test to detect drug abuse. The test is conducted by means of a patch applied to the skin. The patch soaks up sweat and detects the presence of any drugs used during the time it is worn. The patch is designed to remain in place for seven days and is made so that it cannot be removed and then reapplied. It therefore provides a method for testing a subject on a continuous basis for up to a week.[8]

Drug Testing and the Law

One of the first questions that arises in debates over drug testing is a relatively simple one: Is it legal? Can employers force employees to give a urine sample, a hair sample, or some other material from their bodies to be tested for illegal drugs?

In general, there are two answers to that question. On the one hand, laws have been passed and regulations issued at both the federal and state levels permitting such programs. In many cases, those laws place limitations on drug testing in the workplace. They provide a set of regulations that must be observed in such programs. On the other hand, courts have ruled on cases brought before them by both employers and employees attempting to determine the legality of these practices.[9]

Laws and Regulations

Laws dealing with drug testing fall into two categories: those that require testing and those that permit and/or encourage testing. An example of the first category is Public Law 102–240, signed by President George Bush on December 18, 1991. That law requires that any company with even one commercial motor vehicle driver must (1) develop a comprehensive substance abuse policy, (2) educate and train supervisors of drivers, (3) test all drivers for alcohol and illegal drugs, (4) provide drug and alcohol information to all drivers, (5) choose a substance abuse counseling professional, and (6) comply with record-keeping and reporting requirements. These elements are the same as those that had previously been recommended by the U.S. Department of Labor.[10]

An example of the second category of law is the

Drug-Free Workplace Act of 1988. This law requires federal contractors and those who receive grants from the federal government to maintain a drug-free workplace. The law applies only to companies and individuals who have received a federal contract worth twenty-five thousand dollars or more or who have received a grant in any amount. The law contains a number of specific requirements. Among these are establishing an ongoing drug awareness program, publishing a statement pertaining to drug abuse, signing a statement that the workplace will be maintained in a drug-free condition, and obtaining a statement from any employee who previously has been convicted of violating any statute dealing with drug abuse in the workplace.[11]

The federal government has established regulations for drug testing the nation's truck drivers.

The law does not require employers to establish a drug testing program. Ironically, the terms of the act have been used by employers to justify the creation of such programs, even though the act says nothing about this point.

Administrative Orders

Drug testing policies can also be established through administrative orders issued by the president, by governors, by mayors, or by other officials. For example, President Richard Nixon issued an executive order in 1971 that required random drug testing of military personnel. In 1981, President Ronald Reagan extended that order, requiring mandatory testing of all military personnel.[12]

Probably the most important administrative ruling about drug testing is Executive Order 12564, issued by President Reagan in September 1986. This order requires the head of each federal agency to establish a voluntary employee drug testing program as well as a mandatory testing program for employees involved with law enforcement, national security, public health and safety, or the protection of life and property. The order also authorizes mandatory testing in three circumstances: (1) when there is reasonable cause for suspicion that an employee has been using illegal drugs, (2) as part of an investigation following an accident or the discovery of an unsafe practice, and (3) as part of a counseling or rehabilitation program for illegal drug users. Two months later the Federal Personnel

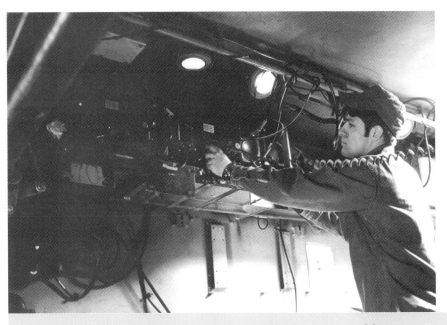

The United States military services now have programs of drug testing for all personnel.

Manual Letter 792–16 was issued. This letter described in more detail the conditions under which drug testing could and should take place, how tests should be performed, and what would happen to individuals testing positive on drug tests.

Some states, on the other hand, have passed laws to protect their citizens from unreasonable drug testing. For example, Montana, Iowa, Vermont, and Rhode Island have passed laws banning all random drug tests (that is, tests conducted without probable cause or reasonable suspicion). In addition, Minnesota, Maine, and Connecticut have passed laws permitting random testing only of employees in certain "safety-sensitive" positions, such as transportation workers.[13]

Court Cases

The legal status of drug testing has been made most clear through dozens of court cases dealing with the issue. One publication discussing the legal aspects of drug testing identified forty-one major court cases involving the issue of privacy.[14] A similar publication reported over four hundred cases in which drug testing was involved at least to some extent.[15]

Landmark Supreme Court cases have been most valuable in determining what kinds of drug testing programs employers may and may not institute. Three of the most important Supreme Court decisions have been *Skinner* v. *Railway Labor Executives' Association* in 1989, *National Treasury Employees Union* v. *von Raab* in 1989, and *Chandler et al.* v. *Miller, Governor of Georgia et al.* in 1997. In the *Skinner* case, the issue was whether the Federal Railroad Administration could require blood and urine tests of all rail personnel involved in serious accidents. In the *National Treasury Employees Union* case, the question was whether the Customs Service could require urinalysis of any employee seeking a promotion or a transfer to a position dealing with illegal drug trafficking, firearms, or classified materials. In the *Chandler* case, the issue involved a state law in Georgia that required candidates for certain public offices to take drug tests.

All of these cases (as well as most other cases)

required the justices to choose between two fundamental rights. The first is the right that American citizens have to privacy and to protection from "unreasonable searches and seizures" by the government. This right is guaranteed by the Fourth Amendment of the U.S. Constitution. The second is the right of the government to protect the health and safety of citizens when that can be shown to be more important than the right of individual privacy.

As an example, Americans are guaranteed the right of free speech by the Constitution. However, that right is not unlimited. In a famous case on the rights of free speech, a Supreme Court Justice remarked that a person had no right to stand up in a crowded movie theater and yell "Fire!" The government is obligated to make sure that public health and safety are not endangered by an individual's free speech.

In both *Skinner* and *National Treasury Employees Union* the Supreme Court ruled in favor of the government. The Court based its decisions on a principle of "special needs" that went beyond the ordinary needs of law enforcement. It ruled that, in certain circumstances, the need to protect the safety of the general public was more important than protecting the privacy rights of individual citizens.[16]

In the *Chandler* case, the Court ruled differently. It said that the state of Georgia had failed to prove that a drug problem existed among state officials, or that those officials performed high risk, safety-sensitive tasks that demanded special protection, or that the law being challenged would provide any protection against the use of drugs by public officials. The court further said that the only case made successfully by the state of Georgia was a symbolic one in standing up against drug abuse. "The Fourth Amendment," the Court concluded, "shields society from state action that diminishes personal privacy for a symbol's sake."[17]

It is important to realize that the decisions in these three cases apply to the actions of government bodies. The Fourth Amendment was written to protect citizens from "unreasonable searches and seizures" *by agencies of the government.* There is no similar constitutional protection against the action of individuals and companies. Essentially, private employers have an unlimited right to carry out drug testing programs in their companies.

3

Drug Testing: An Answer to Problems of Drug Abuse?

Any organization with employees under the age of 40 should think seriously about testing its personnel for drug abuse. For the past 20 years, millions of Americans who began taking illicit drugs as teen-agers have continued their habits as they have entered the work force. . . . There is growing evidence that the use of illegal drugs now rivals alcoholism in its devastating effects on workplace safety, performance, and morale.[1]

Many Americans have concluded that drug testing programs play an important and even essential role in the workplace. In one survey, 78 percent of those interviewed said they supported mandatory drug testing in selected industries, such as transportation and construction. Another 69 percent favored random drug testing in all companies, and 62 percent supported mandatory drug testing for all employees.[2] Proponents of drug testing offer five reasons they support such programs: (1) Drug testing reduces workplace accidents; (2) it increases productivity; (3) it improves corporate morale; (4) it reduces drug use in society; and (5) it supports the goal of a drug-free nation.

Reduction of Accidents

One of the most frequently voiced assertions from those who favor drug testing is that it will reduce the number of deaths, accidents, and injuries caused by workers who have been using drugs. Proponents of testing often cite the Amtrak-Conrail accident described in Chapter 1 as an example of the way in which drug use can result in a horrible accident. There are many other examples of drug-related accidents.

- In April 1987, a bus driver drove his bus into a bridge on the George Washington Parkway in Virginia. One passenger was killed and thirty-two others were injured. The driver later tested positive for cocaine, valium, and marijuana.

- In January 1988, the crash of a commuter airplane in rural Colorado was attributed to cocaine use by the pilot. Nine people died in the accident.[3]

- In January 1987, a switch operator's negligence caused the derailment of an Amtrak train, resulting in the injury of twenty-five passengers. The operator later tested positive for marijuana and one other illegal drug.[4]

Other studies cited by testing proponents seem to show how common drug-related accidents have been in the past. Research by the Federal Railroad Administration in 1987, for example, found that out of 759 railway employees who were tested following 175 different accidents, 29 tested positive for one or more illegal drugs, including cocaine, methamphetamine, and marijuana.[5] Proponents of testing say that examples like these reinforce a common-sense view of the drug abuse problem: People who use drugs are more likely to cause accidents than those who do not.

That conclusion is not quite so simple, however. Raw statistics can not show that drug use actually caused an accident. Remember that drug tests measure the presence of drug metabolites; they do not measure impairment. Also, statistics may not show the extent to which an employee who tests positive for drugs was actually involved in an accident.

How effective is drug testing in reducing accidents in the workplace? According to some experts, testing may be a very effective deterrent! One of the most widely quoted studies on testing and safety in the workplace is the one conducted by Peter Bensinger, former director of the U.S. Drug Enforcement Administration. Bensinger was hired by

Georgia Power (GP) to create a drug testing program at the construction site of a new GP nuclear power plant. Bensinger later described the results of his program:

> We note in our report that lost time accident rates have decreased from 5.41 accidents during 200,000 manhours in 1981 to less than 0.5 accidents in 1985. This remarkable achievement may not necessarily be attributed to the anti-drug program, but increased supervisory attention, drug-policy job-site awareness, extensive drug testing, and management commitment to the anti-drug program have probably been significant contributing factors.[6]

In another study on the effectiveness of drug testing, the number of personal injuries among railway workers fell from 2,234 in 1983 to 322 in the first six months of 1989. This decline was attributed to a more vigorous program of drug testing instituted by the nation's railroads.[7]

Increase in Productivity

The increased number of accidents, say proponents of drug testing, is only the most visible problem associated with drug use in the workplace. In addition, employers are burdened with a number of economic costs by having drug users on their payroll. Again, the argument is consistent with the view of the general public: People who use illegal drugs just don't work as hard as those who do not use drugs.[8]

The extent of those economic costs has long been a matter of contention among those interested in drug testing. Proponents of testing often cite figures such as the following:

- Employees who use drugs are absent from work about three times as often as those who do not use drugs.

- Drug users work only two thirds as efficiently as nonusers.

- Companies pay up to 300 percent more for medical costs, such as rehabilitation programs and health and medical bills, for drug users than for nonusers.

- The cost of workers' compensation claims tends to be about five times higher for users than for nonusers.[9]

One of the most widely quoted studies on drug use in the workplace was conducted by Bruce Wilkenson of Workplace Consultants. Wilkenson estimates that the overall financial cost to an employer for having a drug user on the payroll ranges between $8,000 and $25,600 per year for an employee earning $30,000 annually.[10] Nationwide, the total annual cost to employers for hiring drug abusers has been placed at $46.9 billion, a sum that has been repeated by many proponents of drug testing.[11]

The types of employment problems created by drug-using employees are numerous. They include measurable losses, such as absenteeism, overtime pay, tardiness, sick leave abuse, health insurance claims, and disability payments; hidden losses, such as diverted supervisory and managerial time, poor decisions, friction among workers, damage to the company's public image, wasted time, personnel turnover, and premature death; and losses related to legal claims, such as workers' compensation, equal employment opportunity complaints, disciplinary actions, grievance procedures, threats to public safety, illegal drug trafficking on the job, and security issues.[12]

Corporate Morale

Some corporate executives also claim that having drug abusers in the workplace affects the productivity of nonusers. Nonusers are certainly aware of the drug-using habits of their coworkers. In a recent study conducted by the Gallup Organization for the Institute for a Drug-Free Workplace, four out of ten workers acknowledged that illegal drug use by coworkers "seriously affected their [own] ability to get the job done."[13]

Imagine yourself working on an assembly line, knowing that a worker just before you uses cocaine on a regular basis. You might have good reason to be concerned not only about how well your job is going to be done but also whether your own safety is at risk.

Reducing Drug Use

The potential for reducing drug use in general may be the most fundamental reason for having drug

A Sign Of Integrity.

A quality drug testing program says you care about your employees and your entire community. It can save you money, too. It's just good business.

OML Laboratories is Oregon's first certified drug testing lab. We help our clients design and implement custom programs that work. And we offer fast, accurate results, a nationwide collection network and electronic reporting.

WE CARE about our community.
This workplace is DrugFREE.™

DrugFREE™ is a service of OML Laboratories

OML Laboratories   Call us for information on our DrugFREE™ program, **1-800-826-3616, ext. 8082.**

OML Laboratories 722 East 11th Avenue, Eugene, Oregon 97401

Companies often make clear to employees that they do not condone the use of drugs in the workplace.

testing programs in the workplace. Proponents of drug testing argue that workers are much less likely to use drugs if they know they will be detected.

Perhaps the best evidence for the validity of this argument comes from studies done by the U.S. Department of Defense (DOD). In 1982, the DOD instituted mandatory drug testing in every branch of the military. In studies conducted by the U.S. Navy over the following five years, the rate of positive drug tests among personnel dropped from 47 percent (the rate prior to the mandatory testing program) to 22 percent in 1982, to 10 percent in 1984, and to 4 percent in 1986.[14]

The Symbolism of Drug Testing

Finally, some experts argue that drug testing programs should be implemented by employers to show their support for the antidrug campaign in the United States. In 1994, the American Management Association conducted a survey of Fortune 500 companies that had instituted drug testing programs. The survey showed that about half the companies were uncertain about whether their drug testing policies had any real effects on accident rates, productivity, company morale, or other factors. These companies did report, however, that they regarded preemployment screening "as a statement of the firm's commitment to a drug-free workplace."[15]

A Comprehensive Drug Testing Program

When people think about drug testing programs, they are likely to focus on a single facet of those programs. That facet is usually the collection of urine from an employee and the analysis of that urine for the presence of illegal drugs. But an actual drug test itself is only one segment of a more comprehensive approach to the control of drug use in the workplace.

The National Institute on Drug Abuse of the U.S. Department of Health and Human Services has identified five major features of a comprehensive drug testing program: a policy statement, supervisor training, employee education, an employee assistance program (EAP), and provisions for identifying illegal drug users.[16]

A policy statement should explain what the purpose of the drug-testing program is, what employees should expect from the program, and what happens if and when an employee violates the company's policies. The next stage of the program, supervisor training, is intended to help supervisors recognize behaviors that may suggest illegal drug use on the part of an employee. Supervisors are also shown how to refer those employees for additional counseling and assistance.

Employee education is an important feature of the drug testing program because it is designed ultimately to eliminate the need for drug testing. That is, its goal is to teach employees the risks and dangers of using illegal drugs. Employee education may involve the distribution of materials and information about the specific ways in which drug abuse can harm an individual, hinder that individual's work performance, and damage the company for which he or she works. The educational program may also include special presentations or sessions.

Employee assistance programs are often an important component of a drug testing program. One goal of identifying drug abusers on the job (either by supervisory observations or by drug testing) is, of course, to remove unacceptable employees. Another goal, however, is to help employees deal with their drug problems. EAPs usually include not only the supervisory training programs described but also efforts to encourage drug abusing employees to seek help in a drug abuse rehabilitation program.

Both pro-testing and anti-testing groups generally support EAPs. Anti-testing spokespersons sometimes argue that strong EAPs make drug testing unnecessary. Pro-testing groups point out the costs of EAPs, however. They say it is less expensive for some employers simply to test employees without providing a full range of drug education services.

Thus, drug testing continues to be a crucial part of many drug abuse programs. (The methods used in drug testing were described in Chapter 2.) Tests may be conducted under any one of five circumstances. First, all applicants for a job may be asked to take a drug test. The purpose of such testing is to screen out applicants who have recently used an illegal drug. Drug testing proponents point out that preemployment testing also lets applicants know that a company is serious about having a drug-free workplace. Thus, many drug users may never bother to apply to such companies.

Second, tests may be required of all employees involved in any kind of workplace accident. For example, if a train runs off its track, resulting in the loss of lives, all members of the train crew as well as any employee involved in directing the train's movement can be asked to take a drug test.

Third, drug tests may be given when there is reasonable suspicion that an employee may have been

An employer learns about workplace employee assistance programs that help reduce drug abuse.

using illegal drugs. An employee who is chronically late for work and makes many mistakes on the job is a likely candidate for a drug test, especially if this behavior is new or otherwise unexplained for the employee.

Fourth, drug tests may be given on a random basis to some or all employees of a company. For example, the person in charge of testing may simply draw ten names at random each Monday and ask those employees to take a drug test. Or every person in the company may be tested once a year, with the date for each individual's test scheduled at random. Random testing is most commonly used in safety-sensitive jobs.

Finally, employees who have previously tested positive for illegal drugs and have been referred to counseling or treatment programs may be asked to participate in either regularly scheduled or random follow-up drug tests.[17]

Objections to Drug Testing Programs in the Workplace

The arguments in favor of drug testing programs in the workplace may seem quite convincing. However, critics have raised a number of questions about these arguments. The most fundamental point they make is that the statistics cited by proponents of drug testing are highly suspect. Many of the figures that are repeated over and over again have little or no basis in scientific research.

For example, consider the link between drug use

COLLECTION IDENTIFICATION FORM
Drug & Breath Alcohol Testing

TO BE COMPLETED BY EMPLOYER: NTA COMPANY CODE: _____

_____ uses NTA, Inc. (Nationwide Truckers Association) as a

Third Party Administrator for controlled substance testing. _____ is

sending the following employee to be tested:

_____   _____
(Employee Name)   (Social Security #)

1) ☐ DOT   2) ☐ Urine Drug Screen Collection   3) ☐ Pre-Employment
                           ☐ Breath Alcohol Test   ☐ Random
     ☐ Non-DOT   ☐ Physical   ☐ Reasonable Cause
                           ☐ Other_____   ☐ Post Accident
                                                                    ☐ Return to Duty
                                                                    ☐ Follow-up

on _____ at _____ PM / AM .
      (Date)   (Time Notified)

TO BE COMPLETED BY THE COLLECTOR:

Collector remarks:_____

_____

_____   _____ PM / AM
(Collector Signature)   (Time of Collection)

TO ALL COLLECTORS: Please indicate the employer's NTA company code at the top of the
                              custody and control form.

TO URINE COLLECTORS: Please use pre-printed NTA, Inc. custody and control forms:

       **IF YOU HAVE ANY QUESTIONS PLEASE CALL NTA @ 1-800-452-0030

THIS FORM IS TO BE COMPLETED BY THE COLLECTOR & RETURNED TO THE EMPLOYER BY THE EMPLOYEE.

This form is used in the drug testing of employees.

and accidents in the workplace. One of the most widely quoted statistics is that workers who use drugs are four times more likely to be involved in plant accidents than nonusers. Other statistics show that drug users are two-and-a-half times more likely to have excessive absences and five times more likely to file claims for workers' compensation (for which they receive an average of three times as much money in benefits) than nonusers. As it turns out, these data are based on an informal study conducted by the Firestone Tire and Rubber Company of employees who were undergoing treatment for alcoholism, not drug abuse.[18]

Or consider again the study conducted by Peter Bensinger at Georgia Power (on pages 33–34). Gene Guerrero, executive director of the Georgia office of the American Civil Liberties Union, has reanalyzed these claims and come to a different conclusion. Guerrero points out that Bensinger claims a decrease in accident rates at a new nuclear power plant site from 5.41 to 0.49 cases per 200,000 man-hours between 1981 and 1985. Bensinger claims that a drug testing program he began at the site was probably a "significant contributing factor" to the decreased accident rate. But Guerrero notes that the drug testing program installed by Bensinger did not begin until April 1984. The decrease in accident rates between that time and the end of Bensinger's study was from 0.61 to 0.49 cases per 200,000 man-hours, hardly the dramatic improvement claimed.[19]

The validity of the link between drug use and accidents was also tested in a 1993 review of forty-eight businesses that tested employees before hiring and, in some cases, after accidents had occurred or for such reasons as erratic behavior. The study found the same accident and illness rates among these companies as among companies that have no drug testing program at all. The author concludes that a "pre-employment drug test is mostly an intelligence test—you have to be stupid to get caught."[20]

Reexamining Drug Testing Data

Similar objections have been raised about statements connecting drug use and productivity. For example, the frequently repeated claim that workplace drug use costs the nation between $60 and $100 billion annually was based on a study conducted by the Research Triangle Institute (RTI) in 1982. The institute found that the average household incomes of individuals who had *ever* used marijuana on a daily basis were 28 percent lower than the incomes of people who had not used marijuana daily. Researchers then extrapolated [extended] that finding to all households in the United States and estimated a loss of income of $26 billion due to marijuana use. A final figure of $60 to $100 billion came from the inclusion of drug-related crime and accidents, adjusted for inflation and population growth between 1982 and 1989.[21]

The problem with the RTI data, however, was the information that reviewers often do not mention.

The RTI study also showed that there was no significant difference in household income between *current* users of marijuana (or heroin or cocaine) and nonusers. In 1990, critics questioned Henrick J. Harwood, director of the RTI study, about these data. Did they imply that drug use leads to no economic "loss" at all? he was asked. Harwood, who had in the meantime become Director of Drug Policy for the Bush White House, replied, "You would be on safe ground saying that."[22]

Further data on this issue come from an in-house study of drug use among employees at the Utah Power and Light Company (UPL). That study found that UPL actually spent $215 less per year in health insurance benefits on employees who were known to use drugs than on nonusers.[23]

Given the popularity of drug testing in the workplace and the substantial amounts of money spent on such programs, it is interesting to note how few peer-reviewed studies there are on the effects of drug use on employee behavior. A "peer-reviewed" study is one that has been read and analyzed by other experts in the same field to be sure that it is scientifically sound. One such study followed 180 hospital employees who had been given drug tests prior to their employment. Twenty-two of the employees (12 percent) tested positive for drugs and 158 (88 percent) did not. Researchers found no difference in supervisor evaluations or other measures of job proficiency between those who had tested positive and those who had not. The number

Company medical personnel are often trained to recognize behavior on the job that might suggest drug use by an employee.

of employees who were fired during the study included eleven of the negatives and none of the positives. Researchers concluded that the "study did not find a relation between drug use and job performance."[24]

A later study of 2,537 postal employees found somewhat different results. Researchers found preemployment drug testing results to be "associated with adverse employment outcomes" such as accidents, injuries, and absences. They concluded, however, that the level of risk from hiring drug users was "much less than previously estimated." The difference in the job performances of drug users and nonusers, they said, "may not justify the varied costs involved in establishing a drug-screening program."[25]

The results of one of the most carefully designed studies on this issue was reported in late 1995. Scott Macdonald of the Addiction Research Foundation in London, Ontario, conducted a multivariate analysis of factors affecting workplace injuries. A multivariate analysis attempts to sort out the contribution of many possible factors in producing some given outcome, in this case, accidents in the workplace. Macdonald found that the use of illicit drugs ranked last among twelve variables in contributing to workplace accidents. He concluded that illicit drug use seriously affected the job performances of young male workers only. "An implication of this finding," he said, "is that drug-testing is not . . . justifiable to reduce injuries for females or older age groups."[26]

The relationship between employee morale and drug testing may also be more complex than it initially appears. Without question, most Americans and most workers are concerned about drug abuse. A majority of people approve of testing in the workplace especially if it is "someone else" being tested. But critics point out that drug testing can be a degrading experience.

For example, supervisors of drug testing programs must be careful that any urine sample collected is correctly labeled to avoid mix-ups. They may insist that a neutral observer be present while a subject produces urine for a test. Having someone stand next to you while you complete this task can be an embarrassing and degrading experience. It is not clear, opponents of drug testing say, that such experiences really promote company morale.

Drug Use Trends and Drug Testing

The most fundamental question of all may be whether drug testing has had any effect on drug use in the United States. That question is, of course, a very complex one. Drug use is associated with a great many factors, behavior at work being just one. However, critics do point to one interesting phenomenon. The greatest demand for drug testing programs came in the second half of the 1980s. During that period, proponents of testing argued that the problem of drug use was out of control in the United States. Drug testing was needed to stem the tide of the nation's drug problem. Yet, during that time, abuse of all illegal drugs was decreasing continuously among all age groups. It is difficult to credit the initiation of drug testing programs in the late 1980s for a decrease in drug use that began at least five years earlier.[27]

Ironically, as drug testing programs have become popular, drug use in the mid-1990s, particularly among young people, appears to be on the increase. Proponents of testing say that this increase may be due to a decline in public drug education programs. However, it is also fair to ask how an increase in drug abuse can occur at a time when drug testing in the workplace has become so widely used.

Finally, the most basic claim made by drug testing proponents may well be the potential for identifying drug abusers in American society. If more than 70 percent of all illegal drug users are employed, then a thorough workplace drug testing program should be able to identify significant numbers of drug abusers. Opponents of testing argue, however, that a remarkably small number of drug abusers seem to have been identified in existing programs. For example, former transportation secretary Samuel K. Skinner predicted in 1986 that 8 to 10 percent of the nation's truck drivers, airline pilots, railroad workers, and ship crews would be identified as drug abusers by new testing programs then being designed. In the first year of testing, however, only 177 of the Department of Transportation's 42,215 employees and 67 of its

Maintaining accurate records is an essential part of any workplace drug testing program.

19,029 applicants for employment tested positive, rates of 0.4 percent to 0.5 percent.[28]

Proponents of testing present different statistics on the identification of abusers. The drug company SmithKline Beecham, for example, is one of the world's largest drug testing agencies. It issues a report every six months on the results of their testing programs. In its February 1997 report, SmithKline pointed out that only 5.8 percent of more than 4 million drug tests conducted in 1996 had been positive. That percentage represented a sharp decline from 18.1 percent in 1987. The trend among safety-sensitive transportation workers, however, was somewhat different. The rate of positives in this category actually increased from 2.8 percent in 1993 to 3.6 percent in 1996. SmithKline Beecham pointed out that nearly 60 percent of their positive tests were for marijuana, with another 18 percent for cocaine.[29]

4

The Wrong Answer to a Tough Problem?

Although I strongly oppose illegal drugs and agree something must be done, I feel this is a criminal problem. Testing for all is a further loss of rights and [brings] humiliation, mistakes, and abuse for those who live within the law. I cannot accept any promise that this will not happen.[1]

The above comment reflects the view shared by many workers about the practice of drug testing in the workplace. The most common objections to workplace drug testing are that drug tests (1) violate the right to privacy; (2) are unreliable and often inaccurate; (3) should not be used in place of performance as a measure of an

53

employee's work record; (4) eliminate an important way of offering help to those who are addicted to drugs; and (5) cost far more than is justified by their results.

The Right to Privacy

The Fourth Amendment to the United States Constitution reads as follows:

> The right of the people to be secure in their persons, houses, papers, and effects, against unreasonable searches and seizures, shall not be violated, and no warrants shall issue, but upon probable cause, supported by oath or affirmation, and particularly describing the place to be searched, and the persons or things to be seized.

This amendment compels government agents to show that a crime has been committed before going into a person's home, workplace, or other location to collect evidence against them. For example, a police officer cannot just knock at your door and begin a search of your home. That officer must have reasonable cause to believe that some crime has been committed. And yet, critics say, mandatory drug testing involves collecting evidence against a person without proof that a crime has been committed.

In its position paper on drug testing, the American Civil Liberties Union (ACLU) asks the question, "If you don't use drugs, you have nothing to hide—so why object to testing?" It then answers its own question as follows:

> Innocent people do have something to hide: their

private life. The "right to be left alone" is, in the words of the late Supreme Court Justice Louis Brandeis, "the most comprehensive of rights and the right most valued by civilized men."

Analysis of a person's urine can disclose many details about that person's private life other than drug use. It can tell an employer whether an employee or job applicant is being treated for a heart condition, depression, epilepsy, or diabetes. It can also reveal whether an employee is pregnant.[2]

Some critics further claim that drug testing is part of a growing attempt by the government to expand its control over the personal lives of Americans. Political scientist John Gilliom writes that drug testing is

an innovative means of policing that is part of a broader move to bring social control policy toward an ideal of total surveillance and total crime prevention. While privacy and autonomy are the obvious casualties of such a system, it holds out the possibility of securing almost total compliance with the law in problematic areas like drug use, welfare administration, and taxation.[3]

A similar argument has been made by Leonard H. Glantz, professor of health law at the Boston University School of Public Health. Professor Glantz writes, "In our well-intended desire to stop the flow of drugs into the country and reduce drug use, we are rapidly becoming a nation of suspects. Perfectly law abiding citizens who are under no suspicion of drug use are increasingly being called upon to prove their innocence."[4]

Test Reliability

One of the most highly disputed topics in the field of drug testing is test reliability. The basic questions are How often does a drug test fail to detect the presence of an illegal substance in urine, blood, or some other body fluid (producing a false negative)? And how often does a test indicate the presence of an illegal substance when it is not actually present in the fluid (a false positive)?

These questions are difficult to answer for a number of reasons. First, the answer depends on the type of test conducted. Recall from Chapter 2 that a variety of tests are available for the detection of drug metabolites. Thin-layer chromatography (TLC), enzyme-multiplied immunoassay (EMIT), and gas chromatography/mass spectrometry analysis (GC/MS) are three tests described earlier. The reliability of these tests varies. In general, TLC is less reliable than EMIT, which in turn is less reliable than GC/MS. If a company relies solely on TLC tests, it is likely to get incorrect results more often than if it used GC/MS all the time.

The reliability of drug tests also depends on the skill of the person or the laboratory doing the test. Even though test procedures are highly standardized, they are carried out by humans who sometimes make mistakes. Such mistakes can occur at any point in the testing procedure, from collection of the sample to labeling, storage, or transportation of the sample to the testing laboratory. Mistakes can also occur during the actual chemical test or when reporting the findings of the test.

The ACLU's position on the reliability of drug testing is that

> drug screens used by most companies are not reliable. These tests yield false positive results at least 10 percent, and possibly as much as 30 percent, of the time. Experts conceded that the tests are unreliable. At a recent conference, 120 forensic scientists, including some who worked for manufacturers of drug tests, were asked, "Is there anybody who would submit urine for testing

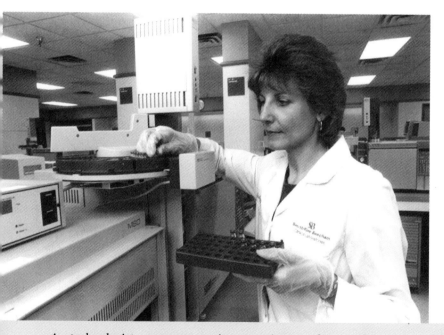

A technologist prepares urine specimens for a drug confirmation test. The laboratory is certified to conduct federally mandated drug tests.

if his career, reputation, freedom or livelihood depended on it?" Not a single hand was raised.[5]

Test reliability changes over time, however. As technology improves, testing techniques become more sensitive. In the 1970s, for example, the commonly used TLC test was just as likely to give incorrect as correct results. Today, GC/MS tests are highly sensitive; they can detect a few nanograms (billionths of a gram) of a substance in a sample. They can also tell if someone has been sitting in the same room with a marijuana smoker, for example. In a properly administered test, however, the opportunities for false positives of this kind are diminished. Some minimum level is set in an effort to prevent the detection of secondhand marijuana smoke, for example.

Another concern of drug testing opponents is that false positive results on drug tests might be assumed to be true. A company may fire an employee or may refuse to hire a prospective employee without having a confirming test performed. Such things are less likely if a second test is used to confirm the positive results of a first test. But in a 1993 study of 177 organizations that do drug screening, only 32 percent conducted confirmatory tests. This finding is troubling because the same study showed that under some conditions, initial tests can be wrong 67 percent of the time.[6]

Finally, drug tests may also be unreliable because the metabolites of some legal drugs or of certain foods are similar to and may be mistaken for those

Some drug tests detect the presence of legal drugs and medications as well as illicit drugs.

of illicit drugs. A person who is legally taking the prescription painkiller codeine, for example, may test positive for opiates on a drug test.

An interesting example is the story of three members of an athletic team from the University of Wisconsin-Madison who tested positive for morphine after a championship competition. The athletes denied having used the drug, however. Research by university personnel eventually uncovered that the three athletes had eaten poppy seed muffins prior to the game. Poppies are the source of morphine, so metabolites from the poppy seeds were mistaken for those of the drug in the postgame testing.[7]

Work Performance or Drug Testing?

One of the basic problems with drug testing, critics claim, is that it focuses on the wrong issue. Testing determines whether an employee has certain chemicals in his or her body, not whether the employee is doing his or her job properly. For example, a person might smoke a marijuana cigarette on Saturday evening and then test positive for the drug during a random test on Monday morning. Does that positive test result mean that the person is unable to do his or her job on that Monday? Also, a person may take a small amount of cocaine on the way to work on that Monday morning. But a drug test taken immediately after he or she gets to work would probably be negative. The cocaine metabolites would not have had sufficient time to get into the bloodstream in a concentration that could be detected. Should employers be confident in either of these cases that drug testing has made the workplace safer for employees?

A fair amount of anecdotal evidence also suggests that drug abuse may not be directly related to employee efficiency in the workplace. In a 1991 article in *The Milbank Quarterly* (a highly respected journal of health care policy), for example, Charles Winick reports on a number of acknowledged drug abusers who hold jobs without having their performance compromised. He cites, for example, a number of physicians who are addicted to illicit drugs:

> There are no reports demonstrating that addicted physicians are more likely to commit malpractice than others. Indeed, the country's largest program

for addicted medical professionals reports that a physician's professional activities represent the last aspect of his or her life to be affected by drug dependence. Drug-using physicians typically have successful and active primary care practices. As O'Donnell noted in his report on addicts in Kentucky, some addicted physicians were described as "the best doctor in town."[8]

One should not conclude, however, that critics of drug testing approve of drug abuse. Their point, instead, is that drug testing should not be used to identify employees who are not doing their work properly. A better way to identify such employees, they say, is through performance assessment, fitness-for-duty testing, or impairment testing. Many testing systems have now been developed. As an example, the company Performance Factors, Inc., has developed a video game that tests hand-eye coordination. Using a joystick, an employee tries to keep a moving cursor positioned at the center of a video screen. The employee's success with the task is compared with a "baseline" score earned on a day that the employee acknowledges himself or herself to be at optimal working conditions. Scores that are lower than this baseline indicate that the employee is not functioning at normal capacity. No conclusion is drawn by the machine itself about the cause of the employee's low performance, though.[9]

Employee assistance programs also can be powerful tools for assessing worker efficiency. Supervisors can be trained to detect workers whose performances are not up to standards. Those workers can then be

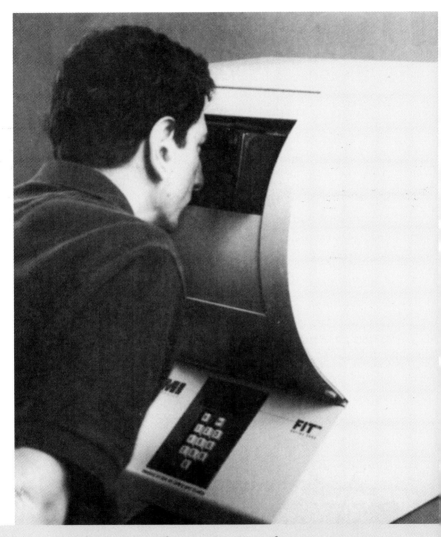

An alternative to drug testing is performance assessment, in which an employee's ability to perform simple tasks is directly measured.

directed into programs that will help them deal with drug abuse problems, if that is the cause of their work problems. Opponents of drug testing point out that this approach is less invasive to workers and more directly related to their job performance.

Keeping Drug Abusers Employed

Why would anyone want to retain an employee who is a known drug abuser? The answer to that question is twofold. First, the employee may be working as efficiently as the nonusers around him or her. And second, retaining the employee may be the best way to ensure that he or she gets help in dealing with addiction.

Suppose that an employee does test positive for an illegal drug and loses his or her job. Chances are that the person may have considerable difficulty finding another job. That person may end up on the unemployment rolls, spending time on the streets, or perhaps doing more drugs. In the end, the fired employee may cost the nation money in a rehabilitation program or a prison when he or she could have had access to counseling programs through work.[10]

Opponents of testing point to a "double standard" in this respect. There is little doubt that many alcohol users and abusers are already employed. These individuals are the cause of at least as many problems as are illicit drug users. Should employers also establish a "zero tolerance" policy and fire anyone known to be an alcohol user or abuser?

Drug Testing Is Too Expensive

Even if drug testing programs do identify some drug abusers, is the cost of these programs worth it? Opponents of testing say no. As an example, a government study conducted in the spring of 1988 found that random urine tests among 30,300 employees produced a rate of only 0.7 percent (212) positives. The cost of these tests was about $15 million.[11] In 1991, a similar result was described by the House Subcommittee on the Civil Service in a report on drug testing of federal employees. Of 28,872 employees tested, 153 (0.5 percent) were positive. The total cost to the government of the testing program was $11.7 million, making the cost per detected positive $77,000.[12] To critics of testing, such results are far too meager to justify the enormous expense of testing.

Examples of Failed Drug Tests

The issue of drug testing often comes down to individual stories. For proponents of testing, the 1987 Amtrak-Conrail train wreck is a cautionary story that demonstrates the need for testing. Those opposed to testing, however, cite stories revealing how individuals' lives have been damaged by drug testing experiences.

> Suitable drug testing meant being forced by a nurse to drop her pants to her ankles, bend over at the waist with her knees slightly bent, hold her right arm in the air, and with her left hand angle a specimen bottle between her legs. She sobbed

and shook, wet herself, and vomited. She was fired for insubordination: refusal to take another test.[13]

I was permitted to wait in the hallway for the results of my test. It was positive for cannabis (marijuana) on two repeats of the field test on the same sample. . . . I took the advice of both the person in charge [of the test] and my attorney, took leave and underwent a complete drug screen test at two different hospitals. . . . Both tests were negative for all controlled substances, both returned results within twenty-four hours and both were performed at my expense. . . . As a toxicologist, I can tell you that . . . we do not test rats the way I was tested for drug use. . . . I suffered a near total disruption to my professional performance, family life, and sleep.[14]

During the 1972 Olympic Games, American long-distance swimmer Rick De Mont was forced to give up a gold medal he had won. In a post-race test, he tested positive to an illegal drug (ephedrine). As it happened, De Mont had been taking an antihistamine prescribed by his doctor before the race. The antihistamine showed up on the drug test as an illegal substance and De Mont's victory was nullified.[15]

Responses to the Anti-Testing Arguments

Proponents of drug testing point to a number of weaknesses in the preceding arguments. In the first place, they say, opponents of testing are wrong in relying on the Fourth Amendment as an argument against drug testing. The Fourth Amendment deals only with unwarranted searches by the federal government, they argue, and not by private companies.[16]

Moreover, the Constitution does not provide absolute protection for a person's privacy. Instead, the Fourth Amendment was written to protect people from *unreasonable* searches and seizures. And in the case of drug abuse, proponents suggest that drug testing can hardly be thought of as an unreasonable search. Given the extent of the drug abuse problem in the United States, they say, it seems reasonable to ask a worker to provide a urine sample for testing.

One writer phrased the argument as follows:

> An employer has a right to prescribe legitimate terms and conditions of employment, even if these intrude on an individual's off-duty conduct. Drug testing is another example of a wide range of tests used to evaluate employees to determine whether they are fit for duty.
>
> For example, public employees routinely are required to submit to fingerprint checks, FBI full-field background investigations, and physical and medical examinations—including compelled urine tests—to determine "fitness for duty." Those who run for public office must file detailed accounts of financial and business matters, and attorneys must pass "character and fitness" exams by providing intimate medical and psychiatric records to character and fitness committees before they may be licensed to practice.[17]

The Supreme Court has apparently accepted this argument. Justice Anthony Kennedy outlined this position in the Court's ruling in the case of *Skinner* v. *Railway Labor Executives' Association*. Kennedy said drug testing can be viewed as a special case when there is "an important government interest" involved, such as protecting public safety. It is true, Kennedy went on, that a person's privacy may be invaded, but drug testing represents a "minimal" invasion of privacy. In such a case, it is not necessary for a tester to have reason to suspect that someone is a drug user. The greater interest of public safety overrides the lesser interest of personal privacy in this case.[18]

Drug Testing Reliability

Proponents of testing also reject the argument that drug tests are unreliable. Of course, mistakes will always be made in any kind of scientific test. But tests are constantly being improved. With each new test, the rate of false positives is reduced. Furthermore, any legitimate drug testing program uses confirmatory tests that are more reliable than urinalysis, which is usually the first test used in a testing program.

In its booklet *The Drug-Free Workplace Employer's Manual*, the National Drugs Don't Work Partnership asks the question, "How reliable are tests?" The answer given is

> Extremely. All testing should be conducted by laboratories certified by the U.S. Dept. of Health and Human Services (DHHS) and all collection, testing, and Medical Review Officer's procedures should be in accordance with DHHS "mandatory

guidelines" for federal workplace programs. This provides the highest level of employee protections and safeguards with regard to specimen collection, chain-of-custody, testing procedures and use of a medical doctor trained in substance abuse and testing procedures to verify "positive" test results.[19]

Robert DuPont, a partner in a professional consulting firm on drug testing, claims, "At the present time, there is no chance of a false-positive result occurring in a well-run workplace drug testing program."[20]

With regard to performance testing of employees, the major question is probably cost. Today, a reasonably reliable urinalysis can be conducted for about $1 per employee, supporters of testing point out. (This cost does not include any confirmatory tests or other EAP elements.) With random testing, that cost usually occurs no more than once every two years. By contrast, performance testing occurs much more frequently, in some cases every day. In addition, the equipment needed to conduct such tests can often be very expensive. However attractive performance testing may appear on paper, it could never cheaply replace urine testing in practice.

Finally, proponents of drug testing say that those who oppose it miss the point by questioning the costs. The cost of drug abuse in the workplace certainly runs into the tens or hundreds of millions of dollars annually. Supporters believe that any program, such as drug testing, that costs a few

Urine tests are less expensive and easier to implement than fitness-for-duty tests.

million dollars per year but also identifies drug abusers in the workplace is very much worth the cost.

Making the Choice

The debate about drug testing in the workplace involves many issues that are still not completely resolved: the privacy rights of employees, the reliability of drug testing, the economic rights of companies, and the cost-benefit value of drug testing. In America's schools and among professional athletes, however, the question of drug testing raises some special questions.

5

Drug Testing in Schools

Today's younger generation is often too accepting of drugs as a part of its life, and adults are too unwilling to implement existing anti-drug laws. With the massive drug problem that exists in our schools today, new legislation is necessary to discourage substance abuse. Cities in Texas, New York, California, and Tennessee have already implemented mandatory drug testing in some of their public schools. Such a program is needed on a national scale. [1]

Schools have been called "the workplace of young Americans." Principals and teachers have been called a boy or girl's "first employer." So it is probably

71

not surprising that some people are asking for drug testing programs in schools. They are expressing concerns not only about the problem of drug abuse in general but also about its spread among younger citizens in particular.

An indication of this concern is the suggestion made by President Bill Clinton in October 1996 that all teenagers applying for a driver's license should be drug tested. Clinton said the government should use the privilege of a driver's license to demand responsible behavior by young people when it comes to drugs, too. "Our message," he went on to say, "should be simple: No drugs or no driver's license."[2]

In his article, "Teenagers Need Drug Testing," from which the quotation at the beginning of this chapter is taken, Brian Noal Mittman lists six reasons that young people should be tested for drugs in schools:

1. Drug testing might deter younger or more immature students from using drugs.

2. Students might avoid using drugs to avoid the embarrassment of being caught.

3. Students might be concerned about their drug use being reported to their parents.

4. Parents who learn about their children's drug abuse would be likely to seek help for this problem.

5. Students who are already drug addicted might seek professional help for their problems if

faced with detection on a drug test.

6. Drug testing would detect heavy drug use in a school, increasing the likelihood that the school administration would actively address the problem.[3]

In many schools and colleges, the issue of drug testing most often focuses on athletics. Students who participate in football, basketball, baseball, or other sports are often expected to pass urinalysis tests to make certain that they are not using illegal drugs or steroids. This issue is related to drug testing in professional sports and will be considered in more detail in the next chapter.

Programs of Drug Testing in Schools

The status of drug testing is somewhat different in schools than in the workplace. While the majority of large businesses now maintain drug testing programs for employees, relatively few school systems do. In a number of cases, proposals for drug testing in schools have been defeated by public opposition or by court decisions. In addition, schools are government institutions. Students are, therefore, protected by the Fourth Amendment.

One example is the drug testing program suggested by the Carlstadt-East Rutherford Regional Board of Education in New Jersey. In August 1985, the board adopted a policy that called for complete physical examinations of all students in the district. All students would be asked to provide urine samples on which a number of tests would be performed, including one looking for evidence of alcohol or drug abuse. Further, the policy stated that any student whose urine tested positive for drugs or alcohol would be assigned to "an appropriate rehabilitation program designed to help the student recognize the danger [of drug and alcohol abuse] and to remedy any problem that exists."[4]

A group of students sued the school district, claiming that the physical examinations constituted an illegal search of their bodies. A state court agreed with the students, stating, "Assuming arguendo [for the sake of argument] that this is strictly and solely a medical examination to inquire into a medical condition, a position which this court does not accept, I would still find that the activities [of the school officials] violate the reasonable privacy expectations of school children."[5]

Other school administrators view drug testing programs as a reasonable way of dealing with a difficult and growing problem in schools. In 1995, for example, the superintendent of schools in Lexington, Kentucky, proposed a systemwide program of drug testing for any faculty member or student suspected of abusing alcohol or drugs. That proposal was not acted upon, however, despite the superintendent's expressed belief that the problem of drug and alcohol abuse constituted a "life-or-death situation." He expressed confidence that the program would eventually win approval by the school board.[6]

These two cases suggest that courts may resist

Drug education for young people may help reduce the need for drug testing later in life.

schoolwide drug testing programs similar to those in the workplace. Judges have been more tolerant, however, of the aggressive pursuit and prosecution of individual drug abusers (or suspected drug abusers) in schools. In case after case, courts have affirmed the rights of schools to search students' property and students themselves for evidence of drug abuse.

For example, the Clearview Junior High School in southern New Jersey had a long-standing policy of searching the hand luggage of students taking part in voluntary field trips. On one occasion in 1990, school officials searched the hand luggage of a student, Brien D., and found no illegal items. Disturbed by the school's practice, however, Brien's mother sued the school district, claiming that the search violated her son's Fourth Amendment rights.

The New Jersey appeals court disagreed with Brien's mother. The basis for the court's decision was a case decided by the U.S. Supreme Court in 1985. In that case, *T.L.O.* v. *New Jersey*, the Court established a two-pronged test for student searches. First, a school must have "reasonable grounds for suspecting that the search will turn up evidence that the student has violated or is violating either the law or rules of the school." The second prong deals with the scope of the search. A search must, the Court ruled, be "reasonably related to the objectives of the search and not excessively intrusive in light of the age and sex of the student and the nature of the infraction."[7] In the case of Brien D., the New Jersey court decided that the student's right to privacy was less important than the school's security interests.[8]

This case typified the position taken by most courts on drug testing in schools. Courts seem to be saying that concern about the nation's drug abuse problem is serious enough to allow schools wide latitude in interfering with the privacy rights of students. Indeed, one attorney involved in such cases observed that "my sense of the climate of the courts in education litigation is that once you say 'drugs,' for practical purposes the case is over for the plaintiff."[9]

The Future of Drug Testing in Schools

What do the cases cited above have to say about the future of drug testing in American schools? The trend would appear to be toward a broader mandate for such programs. But critics of drug testing raise many of the same objections to school programs that they do for workplace programs. In arguing against drug testing in higher education, one writer contends, "Mandatory drug testing without proven cause is profoundly disrespectful. It is a bad lesson for universities to teach and wretched training for citizens."[10]

But one new issue arises when talking about drug testing in schools. Whether one likes it or not, students do not necessarily have all the same rights and freedoms that adults have. For example, the most common type of "drug testing" in schools is locker searches. Teachers and principals routinely open students' lockers without their permission and often without their knowledge. This kind of search is conducted for any number of reasons, from looking for overdue library books to confiscating weapons and drugs.

In cases like this, the question is often asked whether students lose their Constitutional rights at the schoolhouse door. The answer to that question is yes, they sometimes do. Thus far, the courts appear to have sheltered students from the widespread implementation of drug testing that is now common in the workplace. But it is not clear whether or how long that judicial trend will hold.

One reason for this uncertainty is a ruling made by the Supreme Court in June 1995. The case involved James Acton, a student in Vernonia, Oregon. In the fall of 1991, Acton decided to try out for the school football team. He was told that he would have to sign a consent form agreeing to take a test for "controlled substances." Acton declined to do so and then sued the school for violating his Fourth Amendment rights. The Court, in a 6 to 3 vote, ruled in the school district's favor, arguing that mandatory drug testing of student athletes does not violate Fourth Amendment protections against unreasonable search and seizure.[11]

In writing the Court's decision, Justice Antonin Scalia said that the relation of public schools to students is "custodial and tutelary, permitting a degree of supervision and control that could not be exercised over free adults."[12] Justice Scalia's opinion

Drug education programs take many forms.

seems to follow the trend of earlier legal decisions on drug testing. That is, it focuses on safety-sensitive issues rather than granting a broad approval for drug testing of students.

Thus, it is not clear how the Court's decision in this case will apply to other drug testing programs that include nonathletes. In a concurring opinion on the *Vernonia* case, Justice Ruth Bader Ginsburg noted that she was reserving judgment about the broader question regarding the testing of all students in a school or district.

To some observers, the *Vernonia* case signals a "full steam ahead" on school drug testing programs.[13] The school district of New Orleans, for example, announced plans for a pilot program that would require random drug testing of students in two of its schools. At the same time, Kokomo High School in Indiana initiated a plan that required all students leaving campus during the day to submit to voluntary drug testing.

To other observers, *Vernonia* represents a troubling trend toward the narrowing of civil rights for students. In writing about the case in *Phi Delta Kappan*, Perry A. Zirkel, university professor of education and law at Lehigh University, notes, "The Court's decision in this case represents another significant degree in the current swing of the pendulum in the conservative direction. Whether looking at public school search cases or public school student cases more generally, the mediating lens of the judiciary favors school authorities."[14]

6

Drug Testing in Professional Sports

Sports have a very special place in American society. Whether the event is professional football's Super Bowl, the NCAA basketball playoffs, or a Little League baseball game, sports are important to many Americans. Many of those individuals we think of as American heroes are men and women who excel in a field of athletics. High school and college students rally around their athletic teams as symbols of school pride. Professional athletes earn millions of dollars annually by entertaining the general public.

Because sports are so important in our

81

society, drug use among athletes seems especially significant. For example,

> In the summer of 1986, University of Maryland basketball star Len Bias died of cardiorespiratory arrest brought on by the use of cocaine. Bias had been chosen in the second round of the NBA draft only two days earlier.[1]

> In 1991, professional baseball pitcher Steve Howe signed a contract with the New York Yankees. Howe had broken into professional baseball with the Los Angeles Dodgers in 1980. He was named Rookie of the Year for 1980. However, Howe soon began to abuse cocaine. In 1988, his habit was so bad that he was banned from baseball. After being given one more chance by the Yankees, Howe performed brilliantly in 1991. Only months after the season ended, however, he was again arrested for drug use and once more banned from baseball.[2]

> The 1994 Asian Games were rocked with scandal when seven swimmers on the team from China tested positive for anabolic steroids. For a number of years, international sports organizations had suspected the Chinese of using "every dubious Western sporting practice," including the use of anabolic steroids.[3]

Drug Abuse and Testing Programs in Sports

Some people have argued that the issue of drug testing in athletics is no different from that of drug testing in the workplace. After all, for professional athletes, and perhaps for many college athletes, the baseball diamond, the football field, or the tennis court is the workplace. Besides, some observers say, drug abuse is neither more nor less of a problem among athletes than it is among nonathletes. Two comprehensive studies on this question have found little or no significant difference between athletes and nonathletes in their use of illegal drugs and alcohol.[4]

Nonetheless, many sports organizations are keenly aware of their public image. They know that athletes are role models for millions of young Americans and that a "clean" image is essential to their sport. Thus, most professional and collegiate athletic associations have adopted policies regarding the use of illicit drugs by participants in their sports.

The National Collegiate Athletic Association (NCAA) first created its Drug Education Committee in 1973. That committee has developed materials and programs on drug education and testing that are suitable for all athletes, from grade school through university levels. Much of the material originally written for college and university athletics has been adapted for use at lower grade levels.

Today, the NCAA philosophy of drug testing is well developed and outlined in twenty-one separate sections of the association's constitution and bylaws. For example, one section of the constitution reads: "The active member shall administer annually, on a form prescribed by the NCAA Council, a signed drug-testing consent form for each student-athlete."[5]

The procedures by which drug testing is to be conducted are outlined in the NCAA Drug-Testing Program Protocol. The nine sections of that protocol deal with a medical code, organization of drug testing programs, causes for loss of eligibility, methods for selecting athletes to be tested, notification procedures, specimen collection procedures, chain of custody for samples, notification of results and appeal process, and restoration of eligibility.[6] The NCAA tests its athletes for approximately eighty banned drugs. These include stimulants, such as amphetamine, cocaine, and strychnine; anabolic agents, such as anabolic steroids; diuretics, such as bumetanide and chlorthiazide; street drugs, such as heroin, marijuana, and THC; peptide hormones; and substances banned in specific sports, such as alcohol in rifle shooting.[7]

Objections to Drug Testing of Athletes

Just as there are critics of drug testing in the workplace and in schools, there are also critics of drug testing in sports. Some opponents believe that athletes are being held to a higher standard than are nonathletes. Calls for widespread testing of athletes are not appropriate, these individuals say, unless the same kinds of testing programs are required of all workers. For example, Thomas H. Murray, a professor of ethics and public policy, writes the following:

> There is no more reason to screen college or professional athletes than any other students or

employees. Drug education, voluntary testing, and counseling are as appropriate for athletes as for anyone else. But if we genuinely want to help athletes make good moral decisions in their lives—including the decision not to use drugs—then we ought to stop treating them as if they were not morally accountable adults. Screening for pleasure drugs is just one more way of telling them that they are not, and cannot be, responsible individuals.[8]

As with workplace drug testing, one of the most commonly raised questions is the Fourth Amendment issue: Do school, college, and professional sports teams have the right to force an athlete to provide a urine sample for drug testing when there is no specific cause for suspicion?

One of the most thorough analysis of that question is a study conducted by Mark Burzych, professor of law at the University of Michigan. Burzych prepared a summary of all existing legal documents for a sports law seminar held in March 1990. The purpose of the seminar was to see whether the NCAA drug testing program was likely to be ruled unconstitutional in a court of law. His conclusion was as follows:

When the collegiate student-athlete enters a state-supported university, he/she must consent to periodic random urinalyses throughout his/her career conducted by the NCAA. If the student athlete signs the consent form, tests positive for one of the banned substances and wants to appeal the sanctions leveled against him/her based upon Fourth Amendment unreasonable search protections, he/she will have a very tough row to hoe.[9]

In spite of Burzych's view, the issue of drug testing in sports is not entirely resolved. In 1987, Simone LeVant, a member of the Stanford University diving team, sued the NCAA, claiming that urine tests required of her were unconstitutional under the Fourth Amendment. The courts were never asked to rule on LeVant's case since she did not advance to the NCAA finals, where drug testing would have been required. Some legal authorities still consider the issue raised by LeVant to be an "open question."[10]

Performance-Enhancing Drugs

Having compared athletics to the workplace, the fact remains that drugs play a very special role in athletics that they do not usually play in the workplace. The concern among employers is that employees will use drugs that *impair* their productivity. In contrast, the concern of managers, coaches, and sports officials is that athletes may use drugs to *improve* their performance.[11] After all, an athlete's goal is to run or swim faster, lift a heavier weight, function for a longer time, or otherwise "do better" than her or his competitors. Many drugs can help a person do just that. Such drugs are called performance-enhancing drugs.

Many performance-enhancing drugs are entirely legal and are used routinely in sports. Every coffee drinker knows, for example, about the "jolt" provided by the caffeine in a cup of coffee. A driver involved in an hours-long automobile race, for example, might drink lots of coffee to stay alert. Painkillers are also commonly used in sports. Stories are now common of athletes with broken bones being injected with novocaine to allow them to continue playing. Indeed, athletic trainers are constantly challenged with the task of keeping "in the game" players who are injured, ill, or otherwise operating at less than their maximum capacity.

The constant search by athletes for performance-enhancing drugs has turned into a game of cat and mouse between athletes and drug testers. As soon as testers effectively outlaw use of one performance-enhancing drug, athletes look for a replacement. In the 1992 Olympic Games, for example, two American athletes were disqualified when they tested positive for the drug clenbuterol. Clenbuterol is similar to anabolic steroids, for which athletes are routinely tested. One authority on sports medicine speculated that the athletes thought that they could escape detection. At the time, tests for clenbuterol were not as widely used as those for anabolic steroids.[12]

The most common performance-enhancing drugs are a group of substances known as anabolic steroids. An anabolic steroid is a compound with a chemical structure similar to that of testosterone, the hormone responsible for male sexual characteristics. The adjective *anabolic* is used to describe these compounds because, in addition to producing male characteristics, they stimulate the growth of muscle tissue. A person who takes anabolic steroids is likely to gain weight, build muscles, and get stronger.

Anabolic steroids are legal drugs. They can be used to treat hypogonadism in men (abnormal development of the male sex organs) and osteoporosis in women, for example. They are also used in the late stages of breast cancer and in other medical therapies. They can be obtained legally, but only by prescription.[13]

Should Performance-Enhancing Drugs Be Permitted in Athletics?

The changes produced by anabolic steroids are similar to those many athletes hope to accomplish through rigorous nutritional and exercise programs. It is small wonder, therefore, that they are tempted to augment training programs with a "magic pill" (steroids) that could help build body strength and stamina.

The question is whether athletes at any level, from high school through professional sports, should be allowed to take anabolic steroids or other performance-enhancing drugs. Many critics say no and offer a variety of reasons for their stance. In the first place, they point out, medical science has not been able to determine exactly what side effects and long-term effects may be associated with the continued use of anabolic steroids. For example, there is some evidence that prolonged use of steroids results in damage to the liver and the cardiovascular system. These conditions tend to disappear once steroid use has been discontinued, but the possibility of long-term effects still exists.

Second, since steroids are related to the sex hormones, they may also have effects on sexual characteristics. In males, sperm production tends to decrease, sexual organs tend to decrease in size, and sexual drive may be reduced, according to some studies. In females, ovulation and egg development may also be affected. Also, women who use anabolic steroids may begin to develop some male characteristics, such as increased facial hair and a deeper voice.

Third, some researchers also claim that anabolic steroids can cause unexpected mood changes. Such changes appear to result from physiological and chemical changes that take place in the brain as the result of steroid use.

Finally, opponents of steroid use claim that taking chemicals to improve one's athletic performance is simply not ethical. The practice gives the user of steroids an unfair advantage over a competitor who has chosen not to use steroids.[14]

Currently, the consensus of opinion within the sports field appears to be that steroid use should be banned and athletes in any program at the high school, college, or professional level should be tested for steroids. The NCAA, the International Olympic Committee, and the U.S. Powerlifting Federation have all banned the use of anabolic steroids in the sports they oversee.[15]

The use of performance-enhancing drugs is illegal in sports.

Still, some individuals see no problem with the use of anabolic steroids by athletes, and a few even encourage their use. For one thing, they say, coaches and trainers already use a huge variety of legal substances to enhance an athlete's performance. A professional quarterback may be given a shot of novocaine, for example, to relieve the pain of a back spasm. Is that action any more ethical than the use by the same quarterback of an anabolic steroid to increase his strength?

It seems possible that some coaches, managers, team physicians, and trainers may either promote or turn a blind eye to the use of anabolic steroids. After all, the pressure to win at all levels of sports is very high. It would be a surprise if at least a handful of team officials did not make use of a powerful training tool like steroids. On the other hand, it is unlikely that most individuals would acknowledge that they know or approve of such use.

One exception is Dr. Anthony Millar, director of the Research Institute of Sports Medicine at Lewisham Hospital in Sydney, Australia. The key to the question of steroid use, Millar says, is the program under which it is administered. An athlete who wishes to use anabolic steroids must also maintain a nutritional diet and a carefully planned weight-training program. If that athlete's drug use is carefully monitored by a physician, then he or she should suffer no side effects or long-term effects from steroid use. Millar writes that "drugs are not harmful if taken under supervision and I prescribe them for those wishing to take them."[16]

Millar raises one more difficult question about testing for anabolic steroids. Any athlete who uses steroids knows that he or she will eventually be tested for them. Thus, steroid users tend to stop taking the drugs up to six weeks before a major competition. By the time the competition occurs, testing will be unable to detect their use of steroids. What is the value of having drug testing when any user can easily avoid the conditions under which their use will be detected?

Whatever the debate among sports officials and physicians, anabolic steroids retain a powerful appeal for athletes at all levels of competition. If they can provide the extra tenth of a second in speed or the extra pound of force, they may make all the difference in a close competition.

How common, then, is the use of anabolic steroids among athletes? Accurate data on that question is difficult to come by. Athletes may be reluctant to admit to the illegal use of a drug. In addition, tests for anabolic steroids are unreliable unless conducted shortly after their use.

Thus, opinions range widely about the status of anabolic steroids in sports. One authority estimates that steroid use is "on the rise" among professional bodybuilders. Another suggests that use is "down, way down" among college and "elite" athletes.[17] The latter expert then concludes with what may be the bottom line regarding anabolic steroid use: "Most of us agree that scheduled testing isn't that effective for controlling steroids because the advance warning allows athletes to cycle off the drugs. . . . There is an undercurrent of continued attempts to use drugs and to beat the urinalysis and gas chromatograph mass spectrometry tests."[18]

7

Has the Issue of Drug Testing Been Settled?

The issue of drug testing ultimately comes down to the arguments in favor of and opposed to the practice. Proponents, on the one hand, argue that

- drug abuse is such a serious problem in this nation that drastic actions are necessary to deal with the problem;

- the cost to employers of having drug abusers in the workplace is just too high to tolerate; and

- permitting the use of illegal drugs by employees sends the wrong message

93

to the nation's youth about drug abuse.
Opponents, on the other hand, argue that

- drug testing is a violation of the guarantees against unreasonable searches contained in the Fourth Amendment to the Constitution;

- the economic cost of drug abuse in the work-place is greatly exaggerated; and

- drug testing is too unreliable and too costly to justify the results.

It would appear that arguments in favor of drug testing have already won the day in the United States. According to a number of studies, drug testing programs grew dramatically in the decade after 1986. For example, the number of Fortune 500 companies with such programs more than doubled from 18 percent in 1985 to 40 percent in 1991.[1] By 1990, about 96 percent of the top one hundred of those companies had adopted drug testing pro-grams.[2] The latest survey was conducted by the American Management Association in 1994. That survey indicates that about 85 percent of all major firms now have some form of drug testing.[3] By almost any measure, drug testing has become a popular technology among American corporations.

The trends in the data from these surveys are, however, somewhat complex. For example, the majority of the drug tests are being conducted for new applicants, not regular employees. Furthermore, a large fraction of the testing that companies do is required by federal laws and regulations. Without those laws and regulations, the rate of testing might actually have decreased in recent years.[4]

Questions Remain

The intriguing point about these trends is that substantial questions remain about the real need for drug testing in the workplace and the efficacy of such programs in meeting the goals for which they were created. In a 1996 survey of drug testing programs among its member organizations, the American Management Association found that such programs had produced declines of 5 percent in absentee and illness rates, 6 percent in disability claims, 9 percent in accident rates, 2 percent in theft, and 3 percent in employee violence. Moreover, the rate of positive tests was 1.9 percent, a rate that essentially had not changed in a decade. This data raises questions about how effectively and at what cost drug testing programs are operating. Somewhat troubling also was the discovery that less than half the companies surveyed have any drug education program and that one quarter of the companies immediately dismiss any employee who tests positive for drug use.[5]

This survey may support what some authorities have argued for the past decade—namely, drug testing programs have grown in popularity for a number of reasons other than those usually stated by proponents. For example, government efforts to reduce the flow of illegal drugs into the United States have been singularly ineffective. During the 1980s, therefore, the government began to focus more aggressively on reducing the demand for drugs. First Lady Nancy Reagan's "Just Say No" campaign was a particularly prominent feature of that campaign.

However, an important obstacle to the demand-reduction approach was that the majority of illegal drug users were employed and, in general, beyond the reach of the drug law enforcement system. Drug testing in the workplace became, therefore, an important tool in breaking through the protective shield of those employed drug abusers. As one authority wrote,

> Since drug prohibition began early in the 20th century, the government's capacity to identify and control drug users has been limited. Drug abusers coming into contact with the criminal justice system have been imprisoned or forced into treatment, but people who use drugs casually have generally escaped detection and punishment. By testing workers for illicit drugs and denying employment to those who refuse to abstain, workplace drug-testing programs have fundamentally changed the social control of drugs in American society.[6]

This viewpoint is sometimes stated expressly by proponents of drug testing. For example, in 1989, J. Michael Walsh, then director of the Office of Workplace Initiatives of the National Institute on Drug Abuse, wrote, "I believe that a consensus has developed across the country that the worksite is an appropriate place to intervene in the process of individual substance abuse. A responsibility is being imposed on American business to take a more active role than ever before in bringing the national drug problem under control."[7]

The Drug Testing Industry

Another factor in the growth of drug testing in the workplace has been the simultaneous growth of a substantial business designed to service such programs. The drug testing business now has its own professional association (the American Drug Testing Association), at least one professional journal *EAP Digest*), and an annual gross income estimated in 1990 to be between $300 million and $1 billion from the sale of equipment and chemicals used in drug testing.[8]

As a result of this growth, the drug testing industry now has an important stake in perpetuating its own existence. According to one observer, "Whether or not it delivers on its promises to employers, drug testing is likely to remain a common feature of the American workplace."[9]

According to the most recent statistics available, more than 80 percent of all American companies currently test employees either before they are hired or at some time during their employment. Even companies that are not convinced that testing has any real effect on employees who are drug users, on company profits, or on any other measure, continue to test because they think it is "the right thing to do." In addition, companies may decide to test for drugs to protect themselves from possible lawsuits in

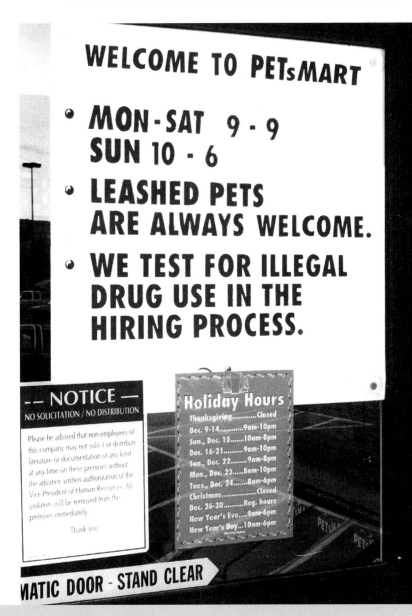

Many companies now conduct preemployment drug tests as part of the hiring process.

case a drug-related accident takes place. Under the circumstances, it seems likely that drug testing in the workplace, in schools, and in athletics will continue—and will probably be used even more widely—for the foreseeable future.

Still, individuals, organizations, and societies do change their opinions on how best to solve social problems. After a decade of drug testing, there is little evidence that testing programs have much, if any, effect on the people who submit to those tests or on the companies that administer them. The only evident outcome of a decade of testing is the development of a massive, multimillion-dollar-a-year business of drug testers—companies that plan, administer, and interpret testing for individual companies.

As with most social issues, the question of drug testing cannot be said to have been settled once and for all. Solutions that held so much promise a decade ago may need to be reassessed in the future. Early failures of drug testing programs may be illusory, with unexpected benefits showing up at some time in the future. Only time will answer this dilemma.

Chapter Notes

Chapter 1. The Drug Problem in the United States

1. D. Gates, "Legacy of a Railroad Disaster," *Newsweek*, May 18, 1987, p. 8.

2. An unidentified "Fabricator of structural steel in Florida with 30 employees," quoted in "Testimonials," *The Drug-Free Workplace Employer's Manual* (Alexandria, Va.: National Drugs Don't Work Partnership, n.d.), p. 7.

3. George Gallup, Jr., *The Gallup Poll: Public Opinion 1995* (Wilmington, Del.: Scholarly Resources, Inc., 1996), p. 185.

Chapter 2. Testing for Illegal Drugs

1. Clayton L. Thomas, ed., *Taber's Cyclopedic Medical Dictionary*, 13th ed. (Philadelphia: F. A. Davis Company, 1977), p. D–64.

2. Office of Applied Statistics, Substance Abuse and Mental Health Services Administration, *Preliminary Results from the 1996 National Household Survey on Drug Abuse* (Washington, D.C.: Department of Health and Human Services, 1997), Table 5A. This document is also available on the Internet at <http://www.samhsa.gov/oas/nhsda /pe1996/httoc.htm> (October 12, 1997).

3. *The Drug-Free Workplace Employer's Manual* (Alexandria, Va.: National Drugs Don't Work Partnership, n.d.), p. 4.

4. Adapted from American Probation and Parole Association, "Drug Testing Guidance and Practices for Adult Probation and Parole Agencies," publication number NCJ 129199 (Washington, D.C.: Bureau of Justice Assistance, July 1991).

5. Hugh Hansen, Samuel Caudill, and Joe Boone, "Crisis in Drug Testing," *JAMA*, vol. 253, no. 16, 1985, pp. 2382–2387.

6. Christopher Frings et al., "Status of Drugs-of-Abuse Testing in Urine Under Blind Conditions: An AACC Study," *Clinical Chemistry*, vol. 35, no. 5, 1989, pp. 891–894. For a good review of drug testing technology, see Lynn Zimmer and James B. Jacobs, "The Business of Drug Testing: Technological Innovation and Social Control," *Contemporary Drug Problems*, vol. 19, no. 1, Spring 1992, pp. 1–26.

7. Tom Mieczkowski et al., "Testing Hair for Illicit Drug Use," *National Institute of Justice Research in Brief*, publication number NCJ 138539 (Washington, D.C.: U.S. Department of Justice, January 1993).

8. "Sweat Test for Drugs of Abuse," *FDA Consumer*, October 1995, p. 5; James D. Baer and John Booher, "The Patch: A New Alternative for Drug Testing in the Criminal Justice System," *Federal Probation*, June 1994, pp. 29–33.

9. A good review of the legal status of drug testing in the United States can be found on the Internet in "Legal issues and cases for drug testing," Texas Workforce Commission, <http://hi-tec.twc.state.tx.us/employer/drugtest.html> (September 12, 1996), and, for Canada, in "TD Bank's Drug Testing to Be Reassessed," Fasken Campbell Godfrey, <http://www.fasken.com/LabEmpTDBank.html> (September 12, 1996), and "Key Provisions of Drug

and Alcohol Policy Struck Down by Human Rights Adjudicator," Emond Harnden, <http://www. emond-harnden.com/entrop.html> (December 6, 1997). Also see a summary of state and federal drug-testing laws on the Institute for a Drug-Free Workplace page, <http://www.drugfreeworkplace. org/catalog.html> (October 12, 1997).

10. *An Employer's Guide to Dealing with Substance Abuse* (Washington, D.C.: U.S. Department of Labor, October 1990). For details of the regulations, see *Federal Motor Carrier Safety Regulations Pocketbook* (Huntersville, N.C.: Nationwide Truckers Association, January 1996).

11. Ibid.

12. Stephen G. Olmstead, "Drug Testing in the Military," in *National Association of State Personnel Executives and the Council of State Governments, Drug Testing: Protection for Society or a Violation of Civil Rights?* (Lexington, Ky.: The Council of State Governments, 1987), pp. 19–20; Paul Mulloy, "Winning the War on Drugs in the Military," in Robert H. Coombs and Louis J. West, eds., *Drug Testing: Issues and Options* (New York: Oxford University Press, 1991), pp. 92–112.

13. *ACLU Briefing Paper: Drug Testing in the Workplace* (New York: American Civil Liberties Union, 1996). Available at <http://www.aclu.org/ library/pbp5.html> (September 5, 1996). Also see Robert DeCresce et al., *Drug Testing in the Workplace* (Washington, D.C.: Bureau of National Affairs, 1989), Ch. 2, "Legal Considerations."

14. John Gilliom, *Surveillance, Privacy, and the Law: Employee Drug Testing and the Politics of Social Control* (Ann Arbor: University of Michigan Press, 1994), case index.

15. DeCresce et al., p. 255.

16. For a detailed discussion of these rulings, see Gilliom, pp. 100–118.

17. U.S. Supreme Court, *Chandler et al.* v. *Miller, Governor of Georgia et al.*, no. 96–126, available on the Internet at <http://caselaw.findlaw.com/scripts> (December 4, 1997).

Chapter 3. Drug Testing: An Answer to Problems of Drug Abuse?

1. Robert L. DuPont, "Never Trust Anyone Under 40," *Policy Review*, Spring 1989, p. 52.

2. The survey was conducted by Opinion Research Corporation of Princeton, New Jersey. Quoted in *The Drug-Free Workplace Employer's Manual* (Alexandria, Va.: National Drugs Don't Work Partnership, n.d.), p. 6.

3. Senator Ernest F. Hollings (D-SC), quoted in *Drug and Alcohol Testing*, Hearing before the Senate Committee on Commerce, Science, and Transportation, 101st Cong., 1st sess., June 15, 1989, pp. 1–2.

4. Robert DeCresce et al., *Drug Testing in the Workplace* (Washington, D.C.: Bureau of National Affairs, 1989), p. 6.

5. Ibid., pp. 6–7.

6. "Plant Vogtle anti-drug program assessment," Bensinger, Dupont & Associates, April 18, 1986, quoted in Gene Guerrero, "The Federal Role: Uncle Sam or Big Brother?" in National Association of State Personnel Executives and the Council of State Governments, *Drug Testing: Protection for Society or a Violation of Civil Rights?* (Lexington, Ky.: The Council of State Governments, 1987), p. 23. But see

later assessments of this study as discussed on page 44.

7. R. W. Taggert, "Results of the Drug Testing Program at Southern Pacific Railroad: Drugs in the Workplace: Research and Evaluation Data," *National Institute on Drug Abuse Research Monograph*, no. 91, (Rockville, Md.: National Institute on Drug Abuse, 1989).

8. A number of studies provide evidence that contradicts the commonsense view of drug use and work efficiency. See the discussion on pages 45–48 later in this chapter.

9. These statistics are often cited by proponents of drug testing. See, for example, Ira A. Lipman, "Drug testing is vital in the workplace," *USA Today*, January 1995, pp. 81–82; Donald D. Bacon, "Business moves against drugs," *Nation's Business*, November 1989, pp. 82+; Peter B. Bensinger, "Drug testing in the workplace," *The Annals of the American Academy of Political and Social Science*, July 1988, pp. 43–50; and "Statement of Gene S. Bergoffen, Executive Vice President, National Private Truck Council," quoted in *Drug and Alcohol Testing*, p. 93.

10. *The Drug-Free Workplace Employer's Manual*, p. 8.

11. H. J. Harwood et al., *Economic Costs to Society of Alcohol and Drug Abuse and Mental Illness: 1980*, Research Triangle Institute, Research Report, (Research Triangle Park, N.C.: 1980).

12. Adapted from "Drugs in the Workplace: Enforcement and Performance," table 2, <http://www.amdahl.com.ext.iacp/psci3.table2.html> (September 28, 1996).

13. *The Employee Drug Education Bulletin*, vol. 1, no. 1, n.d., p. 4.

14. DeCresce et al., p. 7.

15. Glenn Berrien, "Employees Should Not Be Tested for Drug Use," in Karin L. Swisher, ed., *Drug Abuse: Opposing Viewpoints* (San Diego: Greenhaven Press, 1994), p. 122. The original AMA study has not been published, but a summary of its findings is available on the Internet <http://www.druglibrary.org/schaffer/MISC/amtest.htm> (May 29, 1997).

16. A detailed description of the National Institute on Drug Abuse's recommendations can be found in "Comprehensive Procedures for Drug Testing in the Workplace," DHHS publication no. (ADM) 91–1731 (Rockville, Md.: National Institute on Drug Abuse, 1991).

17. For more details on drug testing programs, see *The Drug-Free Workplace Employer's Manual*, pp. 11–14 and *Alcohol and Drug Abuse Provisions in Major Collective Bargaining Agreements in Selected Industries*, Bulletin 2369 (Washington, D.C.: Bureau of Labor Statistics, October 1990).

18. John P. Morgan, "The 'Scientific' Justification for Urine Drug Testing," *Kansas Law Review*, vol. 36, no. 4, 1988, pp. 683–685.

19. Guerrero, p. 23.

20. Dale Feinauer, "Drug Testing Is a Bust," *Health*, September 1993, pp. 18+.

21. For a further analysis of this issue, see Stephen M. Crow and Sandra J. Hartman, "Drugs in the Workplace: Overstating the Problems and Cures," *Journal of Drug Issues*, vol. 22, no. 4, 1992, pp. 923–937.

22. John Horgan, "Test Negative," *Scientific American*, March 1990, p. 18.

23. Ibid.

24. David C. Parish, "Relation of the Pre-employment Drug Testing Results to Employment Status: A One Year Follow-Up," *Journal of General Internal Medicine*, vol. 4, no. 1, 1989, pp. 44–47.

25. Craig Zwerling, James Ryan, and Endel John Orav, "The Efficacy of Pre-employment Drug Screening for Marijuana and Cocaine in Predicting Employment Outcome," *JAMA*, November 28, 1990, pp. 2639–2643; also see Sandra J. Hartman and Stephen M. Crow, "Drugs in the Workplace: Setting Harris Straight," *Journal of Drug Issues*, vol. 23, no. 4, 1993, pp. 733–738.

26. Scott Macdonald, "The Role of Drugs in Workplace Injuries: Is Drug Testing Appropriate?" *Journal of Drug Issues*, vol. 25, no. 4, 1995, p. 717.

27. "U.S. drug abuse level unchanged, survey shows," *Public Health Reports*, vol. 109, no. 6, November/December 1994, pp. 829–830; "1992 household survey shows U.S. drug use decline continues," *Public Health Reports*, vol. 108, no. 5, September/October 1993, pp. 653–654.

28. Harrison M. Trice and Paul D. Steele, "Impairment Testing: Issues and Convergence with Employee Assistance Programs," *Journal of Drug Issues*, vol. 25, no. 2, 1995, pp. 471–503.

29. "Workplace Drug Test Positives Continue to Drop, SmithKline Beecham Reports," on the Internet at <http://www.ndsn.org/FEB97/SKBEECH.html> (December 6, 1997). But note that the data reported here are somewhat internally inconsistent. Also see SmithKline Beecham's home page at <http://www.sb.com/news/dti.html> (October 12, 1997).

Chapter 4. The Wrong Answer
to a Tough Problem?

1. John Gilliom, *Surveillance, Privacy, and the Law: Employee Drug Testing and the Politics of Social Control* (Ann Arbor: University of Michigan Press, 1994), p. 2.

2. *ACLU Briefing Paper: Drug Testing in the Workplace* (New York: American Civil Liberties Union, 1996). Available at <http://www.aclu.org/library/pbp5.html> (September 5, 1996), pp. 1–2.

3. Gilliom, p. v.

4. Leonard H. Glantz, "A Nation of Suspects: Drug Testing and the Fourth Amendment," *American Journal of Public Health*, vol. 79, no. 10, October 1989, p. 1431.

5. *ACLU Briefing Paper*, p. 2.

6. R. Cropanzano and M. Konovsky, "Drug Use and Its Implications for Employee Drug Testing," *Research in Personnel and Human Resources Management*, vol. 11, 1993, pp. 107–257.

7. George L. Landry et al., "Athletes Test Positive for Morphine: A Medical Detective Story," *The Physician and Sportsmedicine*, vol. 22, no. 2, February 1994, pp. 93–95. Also see J. L. Abelson, "Urine Drug Testing—Watch What You Eat!" *JAMA*, vol. 266, no. 22, 1991, pp. 3130–3131.

8. Charles Winick, "Social Behavior, Public Policy, and Non-Harmful Drug Use," *The Milbank Quarterly*, vol. 69, no. 3, 1991, p. 441.

9. See, for example, Harrison M. Trice and Paul D. Steel, "Impairment Testing: Issues and Convergence with Employee Assistance Programs," *Journal of Drug Issues*, vol. 25, no. 2, 1995, pp. 471–503, and B. Butler and D. Tranter, "Behavioral Tests to Assess Performance," in Scott MacDonald

and Paul M. Roman, eds., *Research Advances in Alcohol and Drug Problems, vol. 11: Drug Testing in the Workplace* (New York: Plenum Press, 1994), pp. 231–255.

10. See Glenn Berrien, "Employees Should Not Be Tested for Drug Use," in Karin L. Swisher, ed., *Drug Abuse: Opposing Viewpoints* (San Diego: Greenhaven Press, 1994), pp. 117–123.

11. Stanley Gitlow, "Barbarians at the Gates," *Journal of Addictive Diseases*, vol. 12, no. 2, 1993, pp. 9–21.

12. "Does Random Drug Testing Pay? Don't Count On It," *Investor's Business Daily*, November 1, 1991, p. 8.

13. This episode is reported to have occurred during the Georgia Power drug testing program described above and is found in Philip Weiss, "Watch Out: Urine Trouble," *Harper's*, June 1986, pp. 56–57, as quoted in Gilliom, p. 6.

14. Testimony of Dr. Sandra Thomson, in *Drug Testing in the Workplace*, Hearings before the Senate Committee on the Judiciary, 100th Cong., 1st sess., May 13, 1987, pp. 384–388.

15. Deborah Ackerman, "A History of Drug Testing," in Robert H. Coombs and Louis J. West, eds., *Drug Testing: Issues and Options* (New York: Oxford University Press, 1991), p. 13.

16. See, for example, *The Drug-Free Workplace Employer's Manual* (Alexandra, Va.: National Drugs Don't Work Partnership, n.d.), p. 15.

17. Nanette Rutka Everson, "Drug Testing: It's a Good Idea and It's Legal," in National Association of State Personnel Executives and the Council of State Governments, *Drug Testing: Protection for Society or a Violation of Civil Rights?* (Lexington, Ky.: The Council of State Governments, 1987), p. 72.

18. *Skinner* v. *Railway Labor Executives' Association*, 489 US 602 (1989).

19. *The Drug-Free Workplace Employer's Manual*, p. 15.

20. Robert DuPont, "Medicines and Drug Testing in the Workplace," *Journal of Psychoactive Drugs*, vol. 22, no. 4, 1990, p. 451.

Chapter 5. Drug Testing in Schools

1. Brian Noal Mittman, "Teenagers Need Drug Testing," *Manchester (N.H.) Union Leader*, October 20, 1986, reprinted in Julie S. Bach, ed., *Drug Abuse: Opposing Viewpoints* (St. Paul, Minn.: Greenhaven Press, 1988), p. 117.

2. Alison Mitchel, "Clinton: Use Drugs, Just Say No to License," *The Sunday Oregonian*, October 20, 1996, p. A1.

3. Mittman, p. 118.

4. Quoted in Thomas J. Flygare, "De Jure: Courts Foil Schools' Efforts to Detect Drugs," *Phi Delta Kappan*, vol. 68, no. 4, December 1986, p. 329.

5. Ibid., p. 330.

6. Steve Sheiko, "Drug Testing Debate Engulfs PLD," <http://www.iglou.com/ssheiko/lamplighter/nov95/drugtest.html> (September 12, 1996).

7. *Desilets* v. *Clearview Regional Bd. of Educ.*, 627 A2d 667 (NJ App. 1993).

8. Perry A. Zirkel, "Another Search for Student Rights," *Phi Delta Kappan*, May 1994, pp. 728–730.

9. Quoted in Perry A. Zirkel, "Stripping Students of Their Rights," *Phi Delta Kappan*, February 1998, p. 501. For an extended discussion of this issue, see Zirkel, "Drug Test Passes Court Test," *Phi Delta Kappan*, October 1995, pp. 187–188.

10. Quoted in Thomas J. Flygare, "Mandatory drug tests violate students' rights," in Julie S. Bach, ed., p. 121.

11. Perry A. Zirkel, "Drug Test Passes Court Test." The Court's decision is *Vernonia School District 47J* v. *Acton*, 115 US 2386 (1995).

12. Ibid.

13. Bill Graves, "Vernonia Boy Loses Appeal on Drug Test," *The Oregonian*, May 21, 1996, p. B4.

14. Zirkel, "Drug Test Passes Court Test," p. 188.

Chapter 6. Drug Testing in Professional Sports

1. Jack McCallum, "The Cruelest Thing Ever," *Sports Illustrated*, June 30, 1986, pp. 20–22+.

2. Richard Hoffer, "A Career of Living Dangerously," *Sports Illustrated*, February 3, 1992, pp. 38–41.

3. Alexander Wolff, "The China Syndrome," *Sports Illustrated*, October 16, 1995, pp. 84–88+.

4. William A. Anderson et al., "A National Survey of Alcohol and Drug Use by College Athletes," *The Physician and Sportsmedicine*, vol. 19, no. 2, February 1991, pp. 91–104; Jack A. Bell and Theodore C. Doege, "Athletes' Use and Abuse of Drugs," *The Physician and Sportsmedicine*, vol. 15, no. 3, March 1987, pp. 99–108.

5. Quoted in *1995–96 NCAA Drug Education and Drug Testing Programs* (Overland Park, Kans.: National Collegiate Athletic Association, July 1995), p. 6.

6. Ibid., pp. 10–15.

7. Ibid., p. 9.

8. Thomas H. Murray, "Drug Testing and Moral Responsibility," *The Physician and Sportsmedicine*, vol. 14, no. 11, November 1986, p. 48.

9. Mark Burzych, "Fourth Amendment Analysis and the NCAA Drug-Testing Program: Is it 1st and Goal or Illegal Procedure?" (Overland Park, Kans.: National Collegiate Athletic Association, March 25, 1990, mimeographed).

10. Virginia S. Cowart, "Challenging the NCAA Drug Testing Program," *The Physician and Sportsmedicine*, vol. 15, no. 6, June 1987, pp. 63–64.

11. An interesting question can be raised about the potential use of performance-enhancing drugs in the workplace and the response of employers to such use. That question is analyzed in Nicholas J. Caste, "Drug Testing and Productivity," *Journal of Business Ethics*, vol. 11, 1992, pp. 301–306.

12. Jacqueline White, "Doping at the Olympics: Clenbuterol," *The Physician and Sportsmedicine*, vol. 20, no. 10, October 1992, pp. 19–20.

13. For a good review of the physiological effects of anabolic steroids, see Charles E. Yesalis, ed., *Anabolic Steroids in Sport and Exercise* (Champaign, Ill.: Human Kinetics Publishers, 1993).

14. See, for example, H. A. Haupt and G. D Rovere, "Anabolic Steroids: A Review of the Literature," *American Journal of Sports Medicine*, vol. 12, no. 6, November/December 1984, pp. 469–484; J. L. Krakauer, J. L. Anderson, and R. J. Shephard, *The Year Book of Sports Medicine* (Chicago: Year Book Medical Publishers, 1984), p. 170.

15. Marty Duda, "Do Anabolic Steroids Pose an Ethical Dilemma for US Physicians?" *The Physician and Sportsmedicine*, vol. 14, no. 11, November 1986, p. 173.

16. Anthony P. Millar, "Anabolic Steroids: Should They Be Used to Improve Athletic Performance?" *Current Therapeutics*, October 1985, pp. 17–21, reprinted in Julie S. Bach, ed., *Drug Abuse: Opposing Viewpoints* (St. Paul, Minn.: Greenhaven Press, 1988), pp. 160–161; see also, "Drugs Should Not Be Banned from Sports," by Norman Fost on pages 137–144 in the same book.

17. Don Catlin et al., "Assessing the Threat of Anabolic Steroids," *The Physician and Sportsmedicine*, vol. 21, no. 8, August 1993, p. 37.

18. Ibid., p. 39.

Chapter 7. Has the Issue of Drug Testing Been Settled?

1. Deborah Ackerman, "A History of Drug Testing," in Robert H. Coombs and Louis J. West, eds., *Drug Testing: Issues and Options* (New York: Oxford University Press, 1991), p. 16.

2. S. Feinstein, "Labor Letter," *Wall Street Journal*, August 7, 1990, as cited in Stephen M. Crow and Sandra J. Hartman, "Drugs in the Workplace: Overstating the Problems and the

Cures," *Journal of Drug Issues*, vol. 22, no. 4, 1992, p. 931.

3. "Companies Adding and Expanding Workplace Drug-Testing Programs at Record Pace," *American Management News*, 1993, as cited in Scott Macdonald, "The Role of Drugs in Workplace Injuries: Is Drug Testing Appropriate?" *Journal of Drug Issues*, vol. 25, no. 4, 1995, p. 703. Also see E. R. Greenberg, C. Canzoneri, and T. Straker, *1994 AMA Survey on Workplace Drug Testing and Drug Abuse Policies* (New York: American Management Association, 1994). A summary of this study is available on the Internet at American Management Association, "Workplace Drug Testing and Drug Abuse Policies," <http://www.amanet.org/ama/survey/drugtest.html> (May 29, 1997).

4. See Greenberg, Canzoneri, and Straker, for more details.

5. "Study: Drug Testing Doesn't Deter Use," *USA Today*, October 1, 1996. Available at <http://lcs.usatoday.com/money/company/work/work005.html> (October 4, 1996).

6. Lynn Zimmer and James B. Jacobs, "The Business of Drug Testing: Technological Innovation and Social Control," *Contemporary Drug Problems*, vol. 19, no. 1, Spring 1992, p. 19.

7. J. Michael Walsh, "Drug Testing in the Private and Public Sectors," *Bulletin of the New York Academy of Medicine*, vol. 65, no. 2, February 1989, p. 167.

8. See Robert H. Coombs and Louis J. West, eds., p. xv; Cindy Skrzycki, "Drug-Testing Industry Shows Its Wares," *The Washington Post*, October 27, 1990, p. F1; and Milt Freudenheim, "Booming Business:

Drug Use Tests," *The New York Times*, January 3, 1990, p. D1.

9. Zimmer and Jacobs, p. 20; also see J. Michael Walsh and Jeanne Trumble, "The Politics of Drug Testing," in Robert H. Coombs and Louis J. West, eds., pp. 22–49; Crow and Hartman; Harrison M. Trice and Paul D. Steel, "Impairment testing: Issues and convergence with employee assistance programs," *Journal of Drug Issues*, vol. 25, no. 2, 1995; N. Ben-Yehuda, "The Sociology of Moral Panics: Toward a New Synthesis," *The Sociological Quarterly*, vol. 27, no. 4, 1996, pp. 495–513; and S. Wisotsky, "The Ideology of Drug Testing," *Nova Law Review*, vol. 11, no. 2, pp. 763–778.

Further Reading

Axel, Helen. *Drug Testing: Examples of Corporate Policy, Politics, and Procedures*. New York: The Conference Board, 1990.

Bach, Julie S., ed., *Drug Abuse: Opposing Viewpoints*. St. Paul, Minn.: Greenhaven Press, 1988.

Black, David L., ed. *Drug Testing in Sports*. Las Vegas: Preston Publishing Company, 1996.

Center for Substance Abuse Prevention. *Workplace Drug Testing Programs*. CSAP Technical Report 12. Rockville, Md.: Division of Workplace Programs, Center for Substance Abuse Prevention, 1996.

Coombs, Robert H., and Louis J. West, eds. *Drug Testing: Issues and Options*. New York: Oxford University Press, 1991.

Cornish, Craig M. *Drugs and Alcohol in the Workplace: Testing and Privacy*. Wilmette, Ill.: Callaghan, 1988.

DeBernardo, Mark A. *Drug Testing in the Workplace: Basic Issues, Answers, and Options for Employers*. Washington, D.C.: Institute for a Drug-Free Workplace, 1994.

DeBernardo, Mark A., and Benjamin W. Hahn. *Guide to State Drug Testing Laws: Legislative, Regulatory and Legal Requirements and Developments*. Washington, D.C.: Institute for a Drug-Free Workplace, 1993.

DeBernardo, Mark A., Marci M. DeLancey, and Benjamin W. Hahn. *Guide to State Drug-Testing Laws: Including Relevant Workers' Compensation and Unemployment Compensation Statutory and Case Law*. Washington, D.C.: Institute for a Drug-Free Workplace, 1994.

DeCresce, Robert, et al. *Drug Testing in the Workplace*. Chicago: ASP Press, 1989.

Drug Testing: A Workplace Guide to Designing Practical Policies and Winning Arbitration. Washington, D.C.: BNA, 1990.

Evans, David G. *Drug Testing Law, Technology and Practice*. New York: Clark Boardman Callaghan, 1992.

Executive Knowledgeworks Staff. *Drug Testing in the Workplace: A Resource Manual and Benchmarking Report on Nationwide Practices and Trends*. Palatine, Ill.: Executive Knowledgeworks, 1987.

Fay, John. *Drug Testing*. Boston: Butterworth-Heinemann, 1990.

Gilliom, John. *Surveillance, Privacy, and the Law: Employee Drug Testing and the Politics of Social Control*. Ann Arbor: University of Michigan Press, 1994.

Giordan, Peter. *Drug Testing and the Drug-Free Workplace: A Bibliographic Guide and Reader.* Washington, D.C.: Congressional Research Service, 1990.

Gust, Steven W. *Drugs in the Workplace: Research and Evaluation Data.* NIDA Research Monograph 91. Rockville, Md.: National Institute on Drug Abuse, 1989.

Gust, Steven W., et al. *Drugs in the Workplace: Research and Evaluation Data, Volume 2.* NIDA Research Monograph 100. Rockville, Md.: National Institute on Drug Abuse, 1990.

Gustafson, Katharine. *Drug and Alcohol Testing for Local Government Transportation Employees: The Public Employer's Guide.* Washington, D.C.: International City-County Management Association, 1994.

Kintz, Pascal. *Drug Testing in Hair.* Boca Raton, Fla.: CRC, 1996.

Knopf, Alison. *Special Report on Drug Testing: Drugs in the Workplace Substance Abuse Report.* New York: Business Research Publications, 1991.

Ligocki, Kenneth. *Drug Testing: What We All Need to Know.* Bellingham, Wash.: Scarborough Publishing, 1996.

Macdonald, Scott, and Peter Roman. *Drug-testing in the Workplace.* New York: Plenum Press, 1994.

National Association of State Personnel Executives and the Council of State Governments. *Drug Testing: Protection for Society or a Violation of Civil Rights?* Lexington, Ky.: The Council of State Governments, 1987.

Potter, Beverly, and Sebastian Orfali. *Drug Testing at Work: A Guide for Employers and Employees*. 2nd ed. Berkeley, Calif.: Ronin, 1995.

Reichenberg, Neil. *Drug Testing in the Workplace: An Update*. Alexandria, Va.: International Personnel Management Association, 1991.

Segura, Jordi, and Rafael de la Torre, eds. First International Symposium on Current Issues of Drug Abuse Testing. Boca Raton, Fla.: CRC, 1992.

Swisher, Karin L., ed. *Drug Abuse: Opposing Viewpoints*. San Diego: Greenhaven Press, 1994.

Turkula, William D. *Drug and Alcohol Testing: Advising the Employee*. Charlottesville, Va.: MICHIE, 1994.

U.S. Department of Labor. *Working Partners: Substance Abuse in the Workplace*. Washington, D.C.: U.S. Department of Labor, 1996.

The White House. *The National Drug Control Strategy, 1997*. Washington, D.C.: Government Printing Office, 1997.

Zeese, Kevin B. *Drug Testing Legal Manual: Guidelines and Alternatives*. New York: Clark Boardman Callaghan, 1988.

Internet References

"Bibliography of Workplace Materials" Cesar's Library (University of Maryland)

<http://www.inform.umd.edu:8080/EdRes/
   Colleges/BSOS/Depts/Cesar/wrkp/WORKBIB>
   (September 28, 1996).

Drug-Free Workplace Information Center

<http://www.azstarnet.com/~afdfw/infopg.html>
   (December 6, 1997).

**Indiana Prevention Resource Center,
Indiana University**

<http://www.drugs.indiana.edu/druginfo/
   home.html#testing> (October 12, 1997).

Institute for a Drug-Free Workplace

<http://www.drugfreeworkplace.org/catalog.html>
   (October 12, 1997).

***International Journal of Drug Testing*
(on-line version)**

<http://big.stpt.usf.edu/~journal> (December 6,
   1997).

**The National Clearinghouse for Alcohol
and Drug Information**

<http://www.health.org/workpl.htm> (October 12,
   1997).

Newsgroup on recreational drugs

<http://www.csun.edu/~hbcsc096/dt/dtfaq.txt>
(October 12, 1997).

Privacy Rights Clearinghouse

<http://www.privacyrights.org/fs/fs7-work.html>
(December 6, 1997).

Schaffer Library of Drug Policy

<http://www.druglibrary.org/schaffer/MISC/
amtest.htm> (May 29, 1997).

"Substance Abuse Information Database (SAID)"

<http://www.dol.gov/dol/asp/public/programs/
drugs/intro.htm> (December 6, 1997).

"Urine-test Mailing List"

<http://www.calyx.net/urine-test.html> (October 12,
1997).

"The Worker's Guide to Drug Testing"

<http://member.aol.com/twbrann/drugtest.html>
(December 6, 1997).

Resources

American Civil Liberties Union (ACLU)
132 W. Forty-third St.
New York, NY 10036
Tel: (212) 944-9800
Fax: (212) 869-9065
<http://www.aclu.org>

American Council for Drug Education (ACDE)
c/o Phoenix House
164 W. Seventy-fourth St.
New York, NY 10023
Tel: (212) 757-2100

Employee Assistance Professionals Association (EAPA)
2101 Wilson Blvd., No. 500
Arlington, VA 22201
Tel: (703) 522-6272
Fax: (703) 522-4585
<http://www.ahrm.org/eapa/eapa.htm>

Foundation for Drug Education and Awareness (FDEA)
1301 K St. NW
East Tower, Suite 1010
Washington, DC 20005
Tel: (202) 842-3333
Fax: (202) 841-0011

Institute for a Drug-Free Workplace (IDFW)
1225 Eye St. NW, Suite 1000
Washington, DC 20005
Tel: (202) 842-7400
<http://www.drugfreeworkplace.org>

Join Together
441 Stuart St., 6th Floor
Boston, MA 02116
Tel: (617) 437-1500
Fax: (617) 437-9394
e-mail: info@jointogether.org

National Association of State Alcohol and Drug Abuse Directors (NASADAD)
Drug-Free Workplace Project
444 N. Capitol St. NW, Suite 642
Washington, DC 20001
Tel: (202) 783-6868
Fax: (202) 783-2704

National Drugs Don't Work Partnership
901 N. Pitt St., Suite 300
Alexandria, VA 22314
Tel: (703) 706-0578
(800) 54-CADCA (22322)
Fax: (703) 706-0565

Government Agencies

Center for Substance Abuse Prevention (CSAP)
1010 Wayne Ave., Suite 850
Silver Springs, MD 20910
Tel: (301) 459-1591, ext. 244
(800) 729-6686
TDD: (800) 487-4889
Fax: (301) 459-2919
<http://telnet.ncadi.health.org user-id.new>

Department of Transportation (DOT)
Drug Enforcement and Program Compliance
400 Seventh St. SW, Room 10200
Washington, DC 20590
Tel: (202) 366-DRUG (3784)

Drug Enforcement Administration (DEA)
Public Affairs Section
700 Army Navy Dr.
Arlington, VA 22202
Drug-Free Workplace Helpline: (800) 788-2800

Federal Aviation Administration (FAA)
800 Independence Ave. SW
Drug Abatement Division AAM-800
Washington, DC 20591
Tel: (202) 366-6710
<http://www.faa.gov>

Federal Highway Administration (FHA)
Operations Standards Division
400 Seventh St. NW
Washington, DC 20590
Tel: (202) 366-2981

Federal Railroad Administration (FRA)
400 Seventh St. NW
Washington, DC 20590
Tel: (202) 366-0127

Federal Transit Administration (FTA)
400 Seventh St. NW
Washington, DC 20590
Tel: (202) 366-0188

National Institute on Drug Abuse (NIDA)
Department of Health and Human Services
200 Independence Ave. SW
Washington, DC 20201
Tel: (301) 443-3673

U.S. Small Business Administration
Office of Workplace Substance Abuse Prevention
409 Third St. SW
Washington, DC 20416
Tel: (202) 401-DRUG (3784)

Index

Nixon, Richard, 26

P

PCP, 14

performance assessment.
See work performance
testing

performance-enhancing
drugs, 86–92

perspiration, used in drug
testing, 23

privacy rights and drug
testing. *See* drug testing,
privacy rights

productivity, and drug
abuse, 34–36

Public Law 102-240, 24

R

Reagan, Ronald, 26

reliability of drug tests. *See*
drug testing, reliability

Research Triangle Institute
(RTI), 45–48

S

Scalia, Antonin, 78

Schedule I drugs, 13

Schedule II drugs, 13

Skinner v. *Railway Labor
Executives' Association*,
28, 29, 67

Skinner, Samuel K., 50

SmithKline Beecham,
51–52

steroids. *See* anabolic
steroids

Substance Abuse and
Mental Health Services
Administration
(SAMHSA), 14

T

T.L.O. v. *New Jersey*,
76-77

thin-layer chromatograph
(TLC), 18, 58

tobacco, 14

U

United States Department
of Defense, 37–38

United States Department
of Transportation,
50–51

United States Powerlifting
Federation, 89

urinalysis, 17, 19, 22–23

Utah Power and Light
Company (UPL), 46

V

Vernonia School District v.
Acton, 79–80

W

Walsh, J. Michael, 96

Wilkenson, Bruce, 35

work performance testing,
60–63

Z

Zirkel, Perry A., 80

About the Author

Dr. David E. Newton has written many nonfiction books and textbooks for young adults on science and social issues. Among the titles he has written for Enslow Publishers are *Teen Violence: Out of Control*, *AIDS Issues: A Handbook*, *Population: Too Many People?*, and *Gun Control: An Issue for the Nineties*. Dr. Newton has taught high school science and mathematics as well as several college-level courses. He is now a full-time writer and innkeeper living in Ashland, Oregon.

DATE			
MAY 1 2 '06			